Library of
Davidson College

DIRECTORS IN PERSPECTIVE

General Editor: Christopher Innes

Andrzej Wajda

Andrzej Wajda stands as one of the leading film-makers in contemporary European cinema, although his equally important theatrical achievements have remained less well-known. This book provides the first account and critical evaluation of this Polish director's work for the theatre. Maciej Karpinski examines Wajda's theatrical career focusing especially on such milestone productions as his internationally acclaimed adaptations of Dostoyevsky. Through an analysis of Wajda's aesthetic views and resultant productions, the study also reveals the vital link between his art and contemporary Polish culture. Karpinski is in a unique position to present a study of Wajda. Since 1974 he has collaborated with the director on a number of productions including *The Affair, The Emigrants,* and *Nastasya Filippovna.*

As the most complete study of Wajda in the theatre, this book will enable students and teachers to have a fuller knowledge of this important twentieth-century director. The book also contains a full chronology of his theatrical career as well as photographs from productions.

DIRECTORS IN PERSPECTIVE

What characterizes modern theatre above all is continual stylistic innovation, in which theory and presentation have combined to create a wealth of new forms – naturalism, expressionism, epic theatre, and so forth – in a way that has made directors the leading figures rather than dramatists. To a greater extent than is perhaps generally realized, it has been directors who have provided dramatic models for playwrights, though of course there are many different variations in this relationship. In some cases a dramatist's themes challenge a director to create new performance conditions (Stanislavski and Chekhov), or a dramatist turns director to formulate an appropriate style for his work (Brecht); alternatively a director writes plays to correspond with his theory (Artaud), or creates communal scripts out of exploratory work with actors (Chaikin, Grotowski). Some directors are identified with a single theory (Craig), others gave definitive shape to a range of styles (Reinhardt); the work of some has an ideological basis (Stein), while others work more pragmatically (Bergman).

Generally speaking, those directors who have contributed to what is distinctly 'modern' in today's theater stand in much the same relationship to the dramatic texts they work with, as composers do to librettists in opera. However, since theatrical performance is the most ephemeral of the arts and the only easily reproducible element is the text, critical attention has tended to focus on the playwright. This series is designed to redress the balance by providing an overview of selected directors' stage work: those who helped to formulate modern theories of drama. Their key productions have been reconstructed from promptbooks, reviews, scene-designs, photographs, diaries, correspondence and – where these productions are contemporary – documented by first-hand description, interviews with the director, and so forth. Apart from its intrinsic interest, this record allows a critical perspective, testing ideas against practical problems and achievements. In each case, too, the director's work is set in context by indicating the source of his ideas and their influence, the organization of his acting company, and his relationship to the theatrical or political establishment, so to bring out wider issues: the way theater both reflects and influences assumptions about the nature of man and his social role.

Christopher Innes

TITLES IN THIS SERIES

Adolphe Appia: Richard C. Beacham
Ingmar Bergman: Lise-Lone and Frederick J. Marker
Roger Blin: Odette Aslan, translated by Ruby Cohn
Bertolt Brecht: John Fuegi
Joseph Chaikin: Eileen Blumenthal
Jacques Copeau: John Rudlin
E. Gordon Craig: Christopher Innes
Vsevlod Meyerhold: Robert Leach
Harold Prince: Foster Hirsch
Max Reinhardt: John Styan
Peter Stein: Michael Patterson
Andrzej Wajda: Maciej Karpinski

FUTURE TITLES

André Antoine: Jean Chothia
Peter Brook: Albert Hunt and Geoffrey Reeves
Tyrone Guthrie: Ronald Bryden
Ariane Mnouchkine: Adrian Kiernander
Constantin Stanislavski: Peter Holland and Vera Gottlieb
Giorgio Strehler: David Hirst
Robert Wilson: Arthur Holmberg

Andrzej Wajda, a portrait

The Theatre of Andrzej Wajda

MACIEJ KARPINSKI
TRANSLATED BY CHRISTINA PAUL

CAMBRIDGE UNIVERSITY PRESS

CAMBRIDGE
NEW YORK   NEW ROCHELLE   MELBOURNE   SYDNEY

Published by the Press Syndicate of the University of Cambridge
The Pitt Building, Trumpington Street, Cambridge CB2 1RP
32 East 57th Street, New York, NY 10022, USA
10 Stamford Road, Oakleigh, Melbourne 3166, Australia

Originally published in Polish by WAiF, Warsaw, 1980
First published in English by Cambridge University Press 1989 as *The Theatre of Andrzej Wajda*

English translation © Cambridge University Press 1989

Printed in Great Britain at the University Press, Cambridge

British Library cataloguing in publication data

Karpinski, Maciej
The theatre of Andrzej Wajda. – (Directors
in perspective).
1. Poland. Theatre. Directing. Wajda,
Andrzej
I. Title II. Series
792'.0233'0924

Library of Congress cataloguing in publication data

Karpinski, Maciej.
[Andrzej Wajda – teatr. English]
The theatre of Andrzej Wajda / Maciej Karpinski.
         p.   cm. – (Directors in perspective)
Translation of: Andrzej Wajda – teatr.
Includes index.
ISBN 0 521 32246 4
1. Wajda, Andrzej, 1926- – Criticism and interpretation.
I. Title II. Series.
PN2859.P66W33413 1989
791.43'028'0924 – dc19   88-15979   CIP

ISBN 0 521 32246 4

SE

Contents

List of illustrations	page	ix
Acknowledgements		xii
Andrzej Wajda: an artistic chronology		xiii
1 Introduction: artistic principles and the Polish scene		1
2 Stylistic experimentation: from *A Hatful of Rain* to *Play Strindberg*		14
3 Andrzej Wajda's 'total theatre': *The Possessed, November Night* and *The Danton Affair*		34
4 The dilemmas of liberty: *Abandoned by Reason* and *The Emigrants*		58
5 Madness, love and death: *Nastasya Filippovna* and *Crime and Punishment*		69
6 A reckoning with the past: *Conversations with the Executioner* and *As the Days Pass, As the Years Pass*		91
7 Towards a theatre of politics: *Hamlet, Antigone* and *Easter Vigil*		102
8 Summing up: the theatre of Andrzej Wajda		112
Epilogue		126
Notes		130
Index		133

Illustrations

	Andrzej Wajda, a portrait. (Photographer unknown)	*frontispiece*
1	*A Hatful of Rain*, Gdansk 1959. Johnny (Zbigniew Cybulski) faces drug dealers. Photo: Tadeusz Link	page 15
2	*Hamlet*, Gdansk 1960. A general view of the set at the time of the play within the play. Hamlet (Edmund Fetting) and Ophelia (Elzbieta Kepinska) are seen far right. Photo: Tadeusz Link	19
3	*Two for the Seesaw*, Warsaw 1960. Jerry (Zbigniew Cybulski) and Giselle (Elzbieta Kepinska): a rehearsal photo showing the intimate relation to the audience. Photo: Piotr Baracz	22
4	*The Devils*, Warsaw 1963. Mother Joan of the Angels (Aleksandra Slaska). Photo: Piotr Baracz	25
5	*The Wedding*, Cracow 1963. The Host (Artur Mlodnicki) waves a sabre in patriotic enthusiasm. Photo: Wojciech Plewinski	26
6	*The Wedding,* Cracow 1963. The Poet (Jerzy Nowak, to the right) sees the ghost of Hetman, the traitor (Jan Adamski) in his vision. Photo: Wojciech Plewinski	27
7	*The Wedding*, Cracow 1963. Bourgeois intellectuals being attacked by the peasants. Photo: Wojciech Plewinski	29
8	The same scene in the film version of *The Wedding* (1972). Photo: Renata Pajchel	30
9	*Play Strindberg*, Warsaw 1970. Alice (Barbara Krafftowna), Kurt (Andrzej Lapicki) and Edgar (Tadeusz Lomnicki). Photo: Edward Hartwig	31
10	*Play Strindberg*, Warsaw 1970. General view of the set. Photo: Edward Hartwig	33
11	*The Possessed*, Cracow 1971. Piotr Verkhovensky (Wojciech Pszoniak) and Nikolai Stavrogin (Jan Nowicki). Photo: Wojciech Plewinski	35
12	*The Possessed*, Cracow 1971. Stavrogin's confession (Stavrogin: Jan Nowicki). Matriocha, the girl he raped, is seen in the window. Photo: Wojciech Plewinski	36
13	*The Possessed*, Cracow 1971. Death of Stepan Trofimovich Verkhovensky (Wiktor Sadecki, centre). He is accompanied by Barbara Pietrovna (Zofia Niwinska). Photo: Wojciech Plewinski	39
14	*The Possessed*, Cracow 1971. Piotr Verkhovensky (Wojciech Pszoniak, on the right) forces Kirylov (Andrzej Kozak) to commit suicide, as the 'dark ones' wait in the background. Photo: Wojciech Plewinski	40

x   List of illustrations

15 *The Possessed* (new version), Cracow 1984. Meeting of the revolutionaries. Stavrogin (Jan Nowicki) is seated third from the left, and Verkhovensky (Jerzy Stuhr) first on the left. Photo: Stanislaw Markowski   43
16 *November Night*, Cracow 1974. Pallas Athene (Barbara Bosak) leads cadets to the attack; Jerzy Stuhr (as Lieutenant Wysocki) with the sabre. Photo: Wojciech Plewinski   46
17 *November Night*, Cracow 1974. Photo: Wojciech Plewinski.   48
18 *The Danton Affair*, Warsaw 1975. Robespierre (Wojciech Pszoniak, second from the left) addresses members of the Committee. Photo: Renata Pajchel   51
19 *The Danton Affair*, Warsaw 1975. Danton (Bronislaw Pawlik) before the Revolutionary Tribunal. Photo: Renata Pajchel   52
20 *The Danton Affair*, Warsaw 1975. Robespierre (Wojciech Pszoniak) confronts Danton (Bronislaw Pawlik). Photo: Renata Pajchel   54
21 Danton (Gérard Depardieu) before the Revolutionary Tribunal in the film version, *Danton* (1982). Photo: Renata Pajchel   56
22 *Abandoned by Reason*, Warsaw 1976. Goya (Tadeusz Lomnicki) dressed for the *auto-da-fé* by the Royal Volunteers. Photo: Krzysztof Gieraltowski   60
23 *Abandoned by Reason*, Warsaw 1976. Doña Leocadia (Lidia Korsakowna) as the witch in Goya's vision (Goya: Tadeusz Lomnicki). Photo: Krzysztof Gieraltowski   61
24 *The Emigrants*, Cracow 1976. View of the set. XX: Jerzy Binczycki; AA: Jerzy Stuhr. Photo: Wojciech Plewinski   63
25 *The Emigrants*, Cracow 1976. View of the set. XX: Jerzy Binczycki; AA: Jerzy Stuhr. Photo: Wojciech Plewinski   65
26 *The Emigrants*, Cracow 1976. AA (Jerzy Stuhr) discovers XX's (XX: Jerzy Binczycki) savings hidden in the toy dog. Photo: Wojciech Plewinski   66
27 *Nastasya Filippovna*, Cracow 1977. Prince Myshkin (Jerzy Radziwilowicz) and Rogozhin (Jan Nowicki, on the floor). Photo: Wojciech Plewinski   72
28 *Nastasya Filippovna*, Cracow 1977. Rogozhin (Jan Nowicki) over the prostrate Prince Myshkin (Jerzy Radziwilowicz). Photo: Wojciech Plewinski   75
29 *Crime and Punishment*, Cracow 1984. General view of the set. Raskolnikov (Jerzy Radziwilowicz, centre) enters Porfiry's apartment (Porfiry: Jerzy Stuhr). (Razumichin, on the right: Krzysztof Globisz.) Photo: Stanislaw Markowski   84
30 *Crime and Punishment*, Cracow 1984. Final scene: view of Siberia. Photo: Stanislaw Markowski   85

List of illustrations   xi

31 *Crime and Punishment*, Cracow 1984. Porfiry (Jerzy Stuhr) interrogates Raskolnikov (Jerzy Radziwilowicz). Photo: Stanislaw Markowski   86

32 *Crime and Punishment*, Cracow 1984. Reading of the Bible. Raskolnikov (Jerzy Radziwilowicz), seated at the table, listens to the child, while Sonya (Barbara Grabowska-Oliva) stays back to the left. Photo: Stanislaw Markowski   87

33 *Crime and Punishment*, Cracow 1984. Raskolnikov's confession. In the foreground, display of the material evidence of the crime. Raskolnikov (Jerzy Radziwilowicz) stays in the background. Photo: Stanislaw Markowski   89

34 *Conversations with the Executioner*, Warsaw 1977. Realistic picture of life in prison: Schielke (Kazimierz Kaczor), Moczarski (Zygmunt Hübner) and Stroop (Stanislaw Zaczyk). Photo: Renata Pajchel   93

35 *As the Days Pass, As the Years Pass*, Cracow 1978. 'Family photograph' – the final scene of the second act. Photo: Wojciech Plewinski   96

36 *As the Days Pass, As the Years Pass*, Cracow 1978. Sequence from naturalistic theatre. Young artist Relski (Mieczylaw Grabka and poor servant girl Zosia (Ewa Kolasinska). Phoso: Wojciech Plewinski   98

37 *As the Days Pass, As the Years Pass*, Cracow 1978. Triumphant nouveau-riche Mrs Dulska (Anna Polony, right) forcing her own sister (Izabela Olszewska) to leave an apartment.   99

38 *As the Days Pass, As the Years Pass*, Cracow 1978. Family portrait of the Dulskis. Photo: Wojciech Plewinski   100

39 *Antigone*, Cracow 1984. Chorus dressed as contemporary military commandos. Photo: Stanislaw Markowski   104

40 *Easter Vigil*, Warsaw 1985. View of the audience in the Church of the Lord's Mercy in Warsaw. Photo: Anna Bohdziewicz   109

41 Andrzej Wajda (right) and Maciej Karpinski during rehearsals of *The Danton Affair*, Sofia (Bulgaria) 1978. (Photographer unknown.)   116

42 Andrzej Wajda (right) with actors during a rehearsal of *Crime and Punishment*, Cracow 1984. Photo: Stanislaw Markowski   121

43 *The Vengeance*, Cracow 1986. The Notary (Jerzy Trela) and fearful Papkin (Jerzy Radziwilowicz). Photo: Stanislaw Markowski   127

44 *The Vengeance*, Cracow 1986. Papkin (Jerzy Stuhr, centre) tells his incredible story to the Cup-bearer (Jerzy Binczycki, left) and the Steward. Photo: Stanislaw Markowski   128

Acknowledgements

This is the first book in any language devoted to the theatrical work of the internationally recognized Polish film director, Andrzej Wajda. While a great number of publications on his films is readily available, very little research has yet been done on the other, and equally significant, area of his creative activity. Anyone who attempts to study the subject has therefore to rely mostly on personal observations and opinions.

As for myself, I have been fortunate enough not only to follow the development of the theatre of Andrzej Wajda as a theatregoer and drama critic but also as a close collaborator of the director over a number of years. I have had the rare opportunity to observe his work from the most immediate perspective and I feel privileged to count Andrzej Wajda among my personal friends. This book would not be possible without his generous help.

My thanks go also to Mr Zygmunt Hübner, the Artistic Director of Warsaw's Teatr Powszechny (and formerly of the Teatr Wybrzeze in Gdansk and Stary Teatr in Cracow), the person who first invited Wajda the film-maker to work in the theatre, for his insightful remarks on the Polish version of this book. Professor Christopher Innes deserves my deepest gratitude for his patient guidance and invaluable help in the preparation of the English version. I am also most grateful for expert editorial advice provided by Sarah Stanton and Maureen Street of Cambridge University Press.

The theatre of Andrzej Wajda, one of Poland's leading artists, is a reflection of the situation of Polish culture and – in a broader sense – of Poland itself. If this book can shed some light on these complex problems, my goal will have been achieved.

Andrzej Wajda: an artistic chronology

Wajda's films are indicated only by title and description of genre. Production details are included for theatrical works.

1955   *A Generation* (*Pokolenie*) — feature film

1955   *I Go toward the Sun* (*Ide do slonca*) — documentary film

1956   *Canal* (*Kanal*) — feature film

1958   *Ashes and Diamonds* (*Popiol i diament*) — feature film

1959   *Lotna* — feature film

A Hatful of Rain (*Kapelusz pelen deszczu*) by Michael Vincente Gazzo; set design: Andrzej Wajda; costumes design: Zofia Zuchowska; premiere: 1 May 1959, Teatr Wybrzeze, Gdansk; presented at the first Torun Theatre Festival 1959 (in Poland)

1960   *Innocent Sorcerers* (*Niewinni czarodzieje*) — feature film

The Tragedy of Hamlet Prince of Denmark (*Hamlet*) by William Shakespeare; set and costumes design: Andrzej Wajda; music: Tadeusz Baird; pantomime: Janina Jarzynowna-Sobczak; premiere: 13 August 1960, Teatr Wybrzeze, Gdansk; presented on tour at Brno, Czechoslovakia 1960

Two for the Seesaw (*Dwoje na hustawce*) by William Gibson; set design: Andrzej Wajda; costumes: Zofia Wajdowa; premiere: 23 December 1960, Teatr Ateneum, Warsaw

1961   *Samson* — feature film

Lady Macbeth of the Provinces (*Sibirska Ledi Magbet*) — feature film (Yugoslavia)

1962   *Varsovie* — Polish instalment of the international feature film *L'Amour à vingt ans*

xiv   Artistic chronology

1963   *The Devils (Demony)* by John Whiting: set design: Ewa Starowieyska and Andrzej Wajda; costumes: Ewa Starowieyska; premiere: 2 March 1963, Teatr Ateneum, Warsaw

The Wedding (Wesele) by Stanislaw Wyspianski; set and costumes design: Andrzej Wajda (with Jadwiga Wiesiolowska); music: Jerzy Kaszycki; choreography: Zofia Wieclawowna; premiere: 26 October 1963, Stary Teatr, Cracow

1965   *Ashes (Popioly)* – feature film

1967   *The Gates of Paradise (Vrata Raja)* – feature film (Yugoslavia–France)

1968   *Everything for Sale (Wszystko na sprzedaz)* – feature film

1969   *Przekladaniec* – film for television

Hunting Flies (Polowanie na muchy) – feature film

1970   *Birchwood (Brzezina)* – feature film

Landscape after a Battle (Krajobraz po bitwie) – feature film

Play Strindberg by Friedrich Dürrenmatt; design: Andrzej Wajda; music: Jerzy Maksymiuk; choreography: Gerard Wilk; premiere: 10 March 1970, Teatr Wspolczesny, Warsaw; presented at the international theatre festival Rassegna Internazionale dei Teatri Stabili, Florence 1971

1971   *Pilatus und Andere (Pilate and Others)* – film for television (Germany)

The Possessed (Biesy) by Fyodor Dostoyevsky; adaptation by Albert Camus; stage version: Andrzej Wajda; set design: Andrzej Wajda; costumes: Krystyna Zachwatowicz; music: Zygmunt Konieczny; premiere: 29 April 1971, Stary Teatr, Cracow; presented at the eighth Warsaw Theatre Festival; ninth and tenth World Theatre Seasons, London 1972 and 1973; twenty-first Berliner Festtage, Weimar and Berlin 1977; Holland Festival, Amsterdam 1984; Rencontres Internationales Albert Camus, Angers 1984; and on tour at Zurich 1972 and in Italy (Genoa, Milan, Turin) 1981

1972   *The Wedding (Wesele)* – feature film based on the play by Wyspianski

Sticks and Bones (Kak brat bratu) by David Rabe; design: Andrzej

Wajda; music: A. Lubitski; premiere 26 September 1972, Sovremiennik Theatre, Moscow, USSR

1973   *Der Mitmacher* (*The Partner*) by Friedrich Dürrenmatt; design: Andrzej Wajda and Krystyna Zachwatowicz; premiere: 5 March 1973, Schauspielhaus Zurich

1974   *The Promised Land* (*Ziemia Obiecana*) − feature film

November Night (*Noc Listopadowa*) by Stanislaw Wyspianski; set design: Andrzej Wajda; costumes: Krystyna Zachwatowicz; music: Zygmunt Konieczny; premiere: 13 January 1974, Stary Teatr, Cracow; presented at the tenth Warsaw Theatre Festival 1974 and third Opole Theatre Festival 1977 (award for directing); twelfth World Theatre Season, London 1975; Holland Festival, Rotterdam and Amsterdam 1975; twenty-first Berliner Festtage, Weimar and Berlin 1977

The Possessed by Fyodor Dostoyevsky; adaptation by Albert Camus; stage version: Andrzej Wajda; stage design, costumes and lighting: Krystyna Zachwatowicz; music: Zygmunt Konieczny; premiere: 3 October 1974, Yale Repertory Theatre, New Haven, USA (Robert Brustein, producer)

1975   *The Danton Affair* (*Sprawa Dantona*) by Stanislawa Przybyszewska; set design: Andrzej Wajda and Krystyna Zachwatowicz; costumes: Krystyna Zachwatowicz; premiere: 25 January 1975, Teatr Powszechny, Warsaw; presented at the fifteenth Kalisz Theatre Festival 1975 (award for directing), Opole Theatre Festival 1975 (main prize and award for directing), Belgrade International Theatre Festival (Yugoslavia) 1976 and on tour in Hungary (Budapest) and Romania (Bucarest) 1978

1976   *The Shadow Line* (*Smuga Cienia*) − feature film (Poland−Great Britain)

Man of Marble (*Czlowiek z marmuru*) − feature film

Abandoned by Reason (*Gdy rozum spi...*) by Antonio Buero Vallejo; design: Krystyna Zachwatowicz; music: Zygmunt Konieczny; premiere: 20 March 1976. Teatr Na Woli, Warsaw; won Konrad Swinarski Award (1976); presented at the sixteenth Kalisz Theatre Festival 1976 (award for directing)

xvi Artistic chronology

> *The Emigrants (Emigranci)* by Slawomir Mrozek; design; Krystyna Zachwatowicz; premiere: 24 April 1976, Stary Teatr, Cracow; presented at the nineteenth Kalisz Theatre Festival 1979, international festival Rassegna Internazionale dei Teatri Stabili, Florence 1980 (special award for directing), on tour in Italy (Turin 1980), Hungary (Budapest 1980) and Argentina (Buenos Aires 1982)

1977 *Nastasya Filippovna* (based on *The Idiot* by Fyodor Dostoyevsky) adapted by Andrzej Wajda and Maciej Karpinski; design: Krystyna Zachwatowicz; premiere: 17 February 1977, Stary Teatr, Cracow; presented at the thirteenth Warsaw Theatre Festival 1977; international festivals: Rassegna Internazionale dei Teatri Stabili, Florence 1980; fifth International Theatre Festival in Caracas (Venezuela) 1981; Fringe Festival Edinburgh 1981 (Special Award); Holland Festival, Amsterdam 1984; fifth Theatre Festival in Madrid 1985; and on tour in Finland (Helsinki 1977), Yugoslavia (Dubrovnik 1978), Italy (Turin 1980, Milan and Pontedera 1981, Rome and Palermo 1982), Hungary (Budapest 1980), Argentina (Buenos Aires 1982), England (London 1983), Sweden (Stockholm 1985), West Germany (Karlsruhe 1985, West Berlin 1986)

White Wedding (Biale malzenstwo) by Tadeusz Rozewicz; design: Krystyna Zachwatowicz; premiere: 15 April 1977, Yale Repertory Theatre, New Haven (USA)

Conversations with the Executioner (Rozmowy z katem) by Kazimierz Moczarski, adapted by Zygmunt Hübner; design: Alan Starski; premiere: 22 December 1977; presented at the eighteenth Kalisz Theatre Festival 1978 and the nineteenth Festival of Polish Contemporary Plays (Wroclaw 1978) (award for directing)

1978 *Invitation to the Interior (Zaproszenie do wnetrza)* – documentary film

Without Anaesthetic (Bez znieczulenia) – feature film

As the Days Pass, As the Years Pass (Z biegiem lat, z biegiem dni . . .) by various authors, adapted by Joanna Olczak-Ronikier; co-directed by Anna Polony; design: Krystyna Zachwatowicz and Kazimierz Wisniak; music: Stanislaw Radwan; choreography: Zofia Wieclawowna; premiere 1 April 1978, Stary Teatr, Cracow; presented at the fourteenth Warsaw Theatre Festival 1978, and the Opole Theatre Festival 1979 (award for directing)

Artistic chronology xvii

1979 *The Young Ladies of Wilko* (*Panny z Wilka*) – feature film

Conductor (*Dyrygent*) – feature film

1980 *As the Days Pass, As the Years Pass* (*Z biegiem lat, z biegiem dni. . .*) – mini-series for television based on the stage play

Ils ont déjà occupé la ville voisine (*Oni* [in English 'They']) by Stanislaw Ignacy Witkiewicz (Witkacy); design: Krystyna Zachwatowicz; premiere: 5 February 1980, Centre Dramatique de Nanterre et Théâtre National Populaire de Villeurbane, France

1981 *Man of Iron* (*Czlowiek z zelaza*) – feature film

The Tragedy of Hamlet Prince of Denmark (*Tragiczna historia Hamleta ksiecia Danii*) by William Shakespeare; design: Lidia Mintycz and Jerzy Skarzynski; music: Stanislaw Radwan; pantomime: Zofia Wieclawowna; premiere: 28 November 1981, Stary Teatr, Cracow; presented at the International Theatre Season in Rome 1982 and on tour in Germany (Hamburg 1982)

1982 *Danton* – feature film based on the stage play by Stanislawa Przybyszewska (France)

1983 *Eine Liebe in Deutschland* (*Love in Germany*) – feature film (West Germany)

1984 *Antigone* (*Antygona*) by Sophocles; design: Krystyna Zachwatowicz; music: Stanislaw Radwan; premiere: 20 January 1984, Stary Teatr, Cracow

Crime and Punishment (*Zbrodnia i kara*) by Fyodor Dostoyevsky, adapted by Andrzej Wajda; design: Krystyna Zachwatowicz; special lighting: Edward Klosinski; premiere: 5 October 1984, Stary Teatr, Cracow; presented at the twenty-fifth Kalisz Theatre Festival 1985; Warsaw Theatre Festival 1986 and at the 5th International Festival of Theatre in Madrid 1985; Europaeische Kulturtage in Karlsruhe, West Germany 1985; Berliner Festwoche, West Berlin 1985; Belgrade International Theatre Festival, Yugoslavia 1987 (Main Prize), International PepsiCo Festival in Purchase, NY (USA) 1986; and on tour in Italy (Parma and Palermo 1986, Cagliari 1987), and Israel (Tel Aviv 1986)

xviii   Artistic chronology

1985   *The Chronicle of Love Accidents* (*Kronika wypadkow milosnych*) – feature film

Easter Vigil (*Wieczernik*) by Ernest Bryll; co-directed by Maciej Karpinski; costumes: Krystyna Zachwatowicz; special lighting: Edward Klosinski; premiere: 5 April 1985, Church of the Lord's Mercy, Warsaw; Cultural Award of Clandestine Solidarity 1985

1986   *The Vengeance* (*Zemsta*) by Alexander Fredro; design: Krystyna Zachwatowicz; premiere: 21 June 1986, Stary Teatr, Cracow

1987   *Les Possédés* (*Biesy*) – feature film based on the novel by Fyodor Dostoyevsky and Wajda's stage version (France)

1 Introduction: artistic principles and the Polish scene

Andrzej Wajda's position as a film director is firmly established. His films, such as the early *Ashes and Diamonds* and the recent *Man of Iron* and *Danton*, have won international acclaim and major awards at various film festivals. He is widely regarded as the best contemporary Polish film director and belongs to the inner circle of prominent European directors. Less is known about his concurrent work in the theatre. However, like Ingmar Bergman, Wajda has created works for the stage that are as significant as his films. His Polish productions have been seen in international festivals and on foreign tours, and he has directed work in Italy, France, the United States and the Soviet Union, which has laid the foundations for his international reputation and put him on a par with directors such as Tadeusz Kantor and Jerzy Grotowski.

It must, however, be pointed out that Kantor and Grotowski are primarily creators of their own companies, independent theatre groups with which they experiment, developing their own original theories of theatre. As such, their principles and working methods differ from those of Wajda, who works with ordinary professional companies and in a variety of theatres. Instead of following any particular theoretical concept, he uses the entire panoply of dramatic form and repertoire, achieving widely differing results. In this sense, Wajda's creativity should be likened to that of Peter Stein or Giorgio Strehler rather than to such experimenters as Joseph Chaikin, Julian Beck and Judith Malina, or Grotowski and Kantor.

Grotowski's and Kantor's ideas and the works that are based on them are reasonably well known. Jerzy Grotowski first formed the Teatr Laboratorium in 1962 in Opole and later moved to Wroclaw where he created his 'Poor Theatre', based on his concept that the actor, armed with extraordinary vocal and physical technique, acquired during special training, should be the only important element and creative component in the theatre. Gradually he broke away from the traditional concept of theatre as entertainment. In its place he explored the possibilities of a psychotherapeutic morality theatre, presenting an 'event', a gathering where inhibitions were cast away revealing true, human nature. Typically one of the techniques on which Grotowski based his method of acting was Indian yoga.

In turn, Tadeusz Kantor, a brilliant painter and scenographer, began his career as a director in the underground theatre during the German occupation of Poland. In 1956 he formed his company in Cracow named 'Cricot-2'.

Concentrating at first on producing the work of an avant-garde Polish playwright, S.I. Witkiewicz (writing under the pseudonym Witkacy), above all he promoted the theatre's visual aspects, drawing on his painter's imagination. Kantor was the creator of the first 'happening' in Poland. Later, in the sixties, he began to write his own scripts, using existing literary texts merely as an inspiration. His best-known productions are *The Dead Class* (1975) and *Wielopole, Wielopole* (1980) which showed a fantastical world of memories, dreams and hallucinations conforming only to their own inner, poetic logic. Kantor's productions seem to be pictures come to life in which the main motif is the mystery of death.

Grotowski's Teatr Laboratorium and Kantor's Cricot–2 theatre are the best-known Polish experimental theatre groups. They possess their own theatrical laws and concepts and function independently of mainstream theatre. But in order to define Wajda's more 'traditional' theatre it is essential to place him in the overall context of modern Polish theatre.

At the end of the Second World War the Polish theatrical scene was dominated by those who had achieved popularity and fame before 1939 and they continued to work in the pre-war style. This was either a theatre based on the classics and conventional acting or a more poetic visionary theatre which found its source in Polish Romanticism. In both cases literature was of primary importance, the content being more important than the form. However in 1947, as the new Communist regime consolidated its position, Socialist Realism was imposed as the exclusive and compulsory form in theatre, as in all the other arts. Only plays that fulfilled the requirements of Socialist Realism were allowed to be performed: that is, plays which were naturalistic in form and topical in content. This meant they had to be devoted mainly to 'productivity' and social problems (the class struggle), and presented according to the official political view. Socialist Realism had disastrous effects on the standards and repertoire of the Polish stage. It excluded many of the world's classics, not to mention contemporary West European drama. Little could be achieved in these conditions and many prominent artists either ceased working voluntarily or were forced to do so.

This state of affairs only changed after the political re-shuffle of 1955–6, known as 'the thaw', which culminated in the bloody riots on the streets of Poznan in October 1956. The dogmatic rigours of Socialist Realism were relaxed and Polish culture once again rejoined the international mainstream. Modern dramatic forms such as the Theatre of the Absurd or poetic realism could now be seen on the Polish stage. The new atmosphere of 'political freedom' gave rise to the creative intellectual ferment, which found expression in experimental styles.

A new generation of innovators appeared on the theatre scene. In

Introduction

particular three directors whose influence was to have a profound effect made their debut within a short time of one another: Jerzy Jarocki in 1957, Konrad Swinarski in 1958 and in 1959 Andrzej Wajda, who had already made his mark as a young director in the 'new wave' in Polish cinema. This was the new direction in Polish cinema adopted by Wajda and other young directors in response to the political 'thaw', replacing the dogmatism of Socialist Realism with a romantic impetuousness, especially when portraying Polish history. The most heroic episodes, in particular recent events that had been officially mythologized by the regime – as for example the Second World War – were often depicted with sarcasm and irony, causing much controversy. Wajda's films *Canal* (1956) and *Ashes and Diamonds* (1958) are typical examples of the 'new wave' films.

Konrad Swinarski (born 1929) served his apprenticeship with Berthold Brecht's Berliner Ensemble and on his return to Poland became the chief representative of monumental theatre, which already had a long tradition in Poland. It evolved in the thirties, influenced by the epic theatre of Brecht and Piscator, though without the latter's political consciousness. For example the works of Leon Schiller, its most eminent representative, veered rather towards a poetic vision filled with fairy-tale fantasy. The visual side of these productions was a vital element; they were composed as a series of huge pictures. It was not merely the text that produced thematic significance and atmosphere but the colours, lighting, movement and often the music. Konrad Swinarski is widely considered to be Schiller's 'artistic heir'. His staging of Polish and European classics was noted for a wealth of theatrical devices, inventive design and above all a penetrating, exploratory and original interpretation. In vividly detailed productions such as *A Midsummer Night's Dream* and *All's Well that Ends Well* the unimpeachable heroes suddenly turned out to be cowards, whereas the villains appeared to have feelings after all. Comic episodes would contain unexpected melancholy and the 'funny side' was brought out in the tragic scenes. Above all the characters would be caught up in an ingenious and startling web of ambiguous, psychosexual relationships which influenced all their actions. Swinarski greatly enjoyed filling the stage with real live animals and odd human figures: in *Forefathers' Eve* the 'extras' were a group of authentic Cracovian street beggars, while the characters of *All's Well that Ends Well* were cast as a troupe of body-builders; in *Midsummer Night's Dream*, Puck, as a faun, 'flew' across the stage, leaping into the air from a hidden trampoline. In *Forefathers' Eve* one of the main characters jumped from an actual window in the auditorium. Swinarski achieved international success with productions such as *Forefathers' Eve* by Adam Mickiewicz, part of the World Theatre Season in London in 1973, or the original 1964 West German production of Peter Weiss' metatheatrical

Marat/Sade. Konrad Swinarski died tragically in 1975 in an air crash outside Damascus, on his way to a theatre festival in Shiraz, but his work has continued to have a significant influence on contemporary Polish theatre.

While Swinarski's theatre was monumental and poetic, in the tradition of Polish Romanticism, Jerzy Jarocki (born 1929), is the 'intellectual' of the theatre. Interested less in the visual than in plays that are relevant for their intellectual content, which he manages to convey on stage with great consistency and accuracy, his productions are noted for their precision, both in mathematical design and interpretation. Whereas Swinarski concentrated on the classics, Jarocki works mostly with plays by contemporary Polish writers, from S.I. Witkiewicz (Witkacy) and Witold Gombrowicz to Slavomir Mrozek and Tadeusz Rozewicz. His style is best illustrated by productions such as Witkiewicz's *Mother* and *The Shoemakers* and Rozewicz's *An Old Woman Waits*, which were transformed into commentaries on the disintegration of modern civilization, incorporated in hallucinatory images. For example, in *An Old Woman Waits* human bodies protrude from the heaps of garbage that litter the stage. But beneath this visceral symbolism the tone is clinically objective and controlled: Jarocki takes the part of the cool observer who analyses events without ever becoming involved.

Stylistically Andrzej Wajda stands between Swinarski and Jarocki, and the range of his productions had encompassed both the classics and modern drama, switching eclectically between the two. With his painter's eye and tendency to use violent effects, as in *The Possessed*, he approaches Swinarski, whereas the clarity of intellectual intent and disciplined vision illustrated in *The Danton Affair* and *Antigone* are aspects he shares with Jarocki. His works however are never as analytical and cold. On the contrary, high emotional temperature is a trade mark of Wajda's theatre. In particular he differs from Swinarski in his approach to the art of theatre itself. Swinarski searched for a new meaning in Shakespeare's or Mickiewicz's plays in order to interpret them in a theatrically original and personal way. Wajda seeks parallels between the plays he produces and real life. He not only treats his productions as works of art but uses them to make statements on current controversial events, even using the classics to this purpose. Thus historical perspective and social problems are an intergral part of his theatre, in which political and moral overtones are often more important than the formal aspects.

Irrespective of their similarities and differences, all three directors achieved their greatest successes in the same theatre, the Stary Teatr (Old Theatre) of Cracow, founded in 1781, which moved to its present building in 1799. Although exceptional in its artistic standards, the Stary Teatr is typical of most theatres in Poland from the structural and institutional point of view. All Polish theatres belong to and are administered by the State, either directly or through a local authority. Their activities are therefore not governed by the box-office; the Polish theatre is an institution primarily devoted to Art and free from commercial dictates. At the same time it is entirely dependent on its sponsor in respect of the choice of repertoire and the political tone of the plays performed.

The artistic directors of Polish theatres are usually well-known stage directors or, more rarely, actors. Although many of them impress their personality on their company to such a degree that their personal style literally takes over, most companies hold with the principle of maintaining variety not only in repertoire but also in style. The character of the individual productions mounted by any given troupe can therefore change drastically depending on the personality of a particular stage director.

Most Polish stages are repertory theatres. They have resident companies whose members perform varied roles in a number of concurrent productions. The repertoire is usually wide, covering all styles and origins, from Sophocles or Shakespeare to Pinter or Mrozek. Several different plays are performed each week on alternate days, making heavy demands on the actors in terms of adaptability, and also contributing to their education. An actor is engaged for a season, after which he may, if he wishes, join another theatre company. Nevertheless, many actors attach themselves permanently to one theatre and, as a result, some have very stable companies. The Stary Teatr can boast actors who have worked there for ten years or more. These actors have all had the opportunity of working with a variety of different directors, including major figures such as Swinarski, Jarocki and Wajda. The directors enjoy returning to the same companies in which they feel at home, to work with actors whom they have grown to know. It is this which explains the exceptionally high standard of acting achieved at the Stary Teatr.

It is no accident that, paradoxically, none of these three directors has ever had his own company or held the post of artistic director of any theatre, despite their strong ties with the Stary Teatr. By directing different companies on stages throughout the country and dealing with an assortment of actors they have extended their range and established general artistic standards. Wajda has staged major productions in Gdansk and Warsaw as well as in Cracow, and in these places he would come across actors he had worked with in the past who had moved from one company to another in the interim. Since there is no strict division in Poland between film actors and theatre actors, Wajda has made liberal use in his films of those who have appeared in his stage productions. In spite of the fact that he has never had his own company, unlike Grotowski or Kantor, Wajda nevertheless brought together specific groups of actors during various stages in his career, as well as creating, metaphorically, his own 'theatre' through his individuality of style. It is this 'theatre' which is the subject of the present work.

The theatre plays a role in Polish society which has little to do with mere entertainment. Its prestigious social function is defined by the historical fact that throughout the period when the country was partitioned — from the close of the eighteenth century until 1918 — the theatre was practically the only place in which the Poles could cultivate their national culture. This gave rise to the notion of the theatre's political and moral mission, a notion which continues to determine the direction in which it moves today. As an artist who is particularly sensitive to national traditions, Andrzej Wajda understands perfectly what Polish society expects from the theatre, namely a conscientious voice which can take up historical or ethical issues and discuss the most fundamental human and national problems. For Poles, the theatre is at once a school, a library, a political forum, even a temple, and only secondarily a place of recreation. It is taken seriously by the public and approaches its moral and social obligations with gravity.

This relationship with the theatre is upheld by the dramatic literature to which it has given rise. The Polish theatre takes its repertoire from the universal classics and from the Polish dramatic tradition born of the Romantic Movement. The plays of the nineteenth-century Romantic poets, Adam Mickiewicz, Juliusz Slowacki and Zygmunt Krasinski, revered as the 'bards of the Polish nation', and of their successor, Stanislaw Wyspianski, still form the basic repertoire of Polish theatres, providing the point of departure from which all other endeavours are undertaken. As a result, the vital trend in Polish theatre, as in Polish culture in general, remains the Romantic tradition, which combines nationalism, mysticism, messianism and religion expressed in a lofty yet gloomy poesy. The surviving dominance of this tradition means that every Polish artist today must make a radical choice between conformism or defiance of it.

Andrzej Wajda is one of the most original heirs to the Romantic tradition. In keeping with this tradition, he is an impulsive and inconsistent artist, relying on intuition rather than on preconceived theories. He is a restless director continually staking out new horizons for his own creativity.

His varied creative activities do not facilitate the task of studying his work. Each element of his artistic biography must be viewed in the light of others. These are often highly disparate in content and style, so the thread must be followed through an assortment of material, much of it belonging to separate areas of artistic experience. Yet it would be a great mistake to survey Andrzej Wajda's theatrical work on its own, apart from the rest of his ever-expanding creative output. It is essential to follow, even if only in general terms, the whole of his artistic biography in the context of what interests us here, namely his theatre work.

Introduction

Born in Suwalki on 6 March 1926, Wajda studied painting at the Cracow Academy of Fine Arts, and later film-making at the Lodz Film School, from which he graduated in 1953. In the course of these studies he shot one brief feature film, *The Wicked Boy*, based on a short story by Chekhov, as well as two documentaries, *The Ilza Ceramics* and *While You Sleep*. On completing his studies he followed the accepted course of gaining experience as an assistant director, and although he did not work for long in this capacity, it is worth noting that his apprenticeship in 1954 was spent at the side of Aleksander Ford, known for his films depicting the tragic fate of Polish Jews during the war. In the following year Wajda made his own debut as a film-maker with *A Generation*, which had a immediate impact and provided the foundations for the nascent 'Polish School' in cinema.

At that point Wajda had little respect for the stage, since the traditional style of presentation that characterized pre-1956 Polish theatre seemed irrelevant to current political and social problems:

When I began my studies at the Academy of Fine Arts in Cracow in 1946, the theatre belonged to the actors ... I did not think of becoming a director, I believed in painting ... On the whole, the theatre of the day did not arouse any enthusiasm in me. The actors were entrancing, but all the other aspects were unmemorable. I then moved to Lodz, but the theatre there did little more to kindle my interest ... My dissatisfaction was confirmed by the arrival of productions from abroad. Primarily, *Titus Andronicus*, *The Servant of Two Masters* by Goldoni under the directorship of Strehler, and Brecht's *Mother Courage*. These convinced me that an alternative form of theatre exists out there in the world and that it is capable of being much more intense. Looking back now I think that my views were provoked by the concept of theatre existing at that time, and which we suffer under to this day: that theatre is a place of high ideals, a sort of salon where gestures are more precise, voices more melodious, and where people behave more elegantly than in real life (nothing could have been more false and less interesting for me at that time). I think that maybe I was so opposed to that convention of propriety, elegance and good taste because my films seemed to portray the very opposite.[1]

Wajda made his debut in the theatre in 1959 in Gdansk with *A Hatful of Rain* by Michael Gazzo, a realistic, psychological American drama about drug addiction, premiered in New York in 1955. He had already made his famous films *Canal* and *Ashes and Diamonds*, and from then on the paths of his creative work in both theatre and film interweave. What is more, specific parallels can be observed in the development of his work in both areas, despite the very different demands of each art form.

His films can be, broadly speaking, segregated into several 'periods' which are marked not only by changes in characteristic details of style and by particular moods, but also by, as it were, a vacillation of artistic intent, which resulted in an uneven standard. Thus the First Period at the end of the fifties embraces on one hand his brilliant debut, and on the other his fourth film *Lotna* (1959). The title being the name of a horse whose experiences in battles between the Polish cavalry and the Germans in 1939 provides the story-line, this work contrasted with the blunt realism of his better-known war films from this early period. Where they were in black and white, giving a harsh documentary tone, *Lotna* was the first Polish film in colour, a technical choice that underlined its philosophical symbolism. During the sixties he made films that were not only very different in style and subject, but uneven in quality. Next to the celebrated *Ashes*(1965), a Napoleonic saga based on the popular yet controversial Polish novel by S. Zeromski written in 1904, we have two treatments of classical material, *Lady Macbeth of the Provinces* and *Samson* (both 1961), neither of which was altogether successful. These comprise his 'Second Period' which lasted until he began the film *Hunting Flies*. Stylistically and thematically this marked the transition to his next phase, and *Everything for Sale*, a film shown in the same year, 1969, definitely belongs to the 'Third Period', which is marked by such exceptional works as *Birchwood* (1970), *Landscape after a Battle* (1970), *Pilate and Others* (1971), *The Wedding* (1972), *The Promised Land* (1974), *Man of Marble* (1976), *Without Anaesthetic* (1978), *The Young Ladies of Wilko* (1979), *Man of Iron* (1981) and, most recently, *Danton* (1982).

So there was in Wajda's development a period of 'Sturm und Drang' giving rise to films that were a reckoning with his own youth and that of his generation. Their form was dictated by clearly defined political thoughts and emotional intensity. Then came a second period of vacillation and indecision apparent in the story-line as well as in form. In the 'Third Period' of full creative maturity his style crystallizes, while the film's subject ceases to offer resistance to its author. Form and story-line are fully integrated to serve Wajda's artistic ideas.

The same pattern can be observed in Wajda's theatrical work. His involvement with the stage only occurs towards the end of his first film phase, with the hit *A Hatful of Rain*, then *Hamlet* in Gdansk and *Two for the Seesaw* in Warsaw, both in 1960. These productions mark a period of training, of stylistic exploration. The 'Second Period' contains one flawed production of *The Wedding* in Cracow, and an abortive one of John Whiting's *The Devils* (both 1963) which caused Wajda to leave the theatre altogether. However, with his third film phase, he returns to produce his most famous and significant works in the theatre: *The Possessed* (1971), *November Night* (1974), *The Danton Affair* (1975), *Nastasya Filippovna* (1977), *Antigone* (1984), and *Crime and Punishment* (also 1984).

If we treat Wajda's abundant creative output as a whole, not separating his plays from his films, we notice that the dominant characteristics make up a rich and varied mosaic – its diversity and variety are its strength. Wajda is fascinated by the themes of great Polish literature (two versions of Wyspianski's *The Wedding*, Zeromski's *Ashes* and Wyspianski's *November*

Introduction

Night), by international works encompassing universal problems of humanity (Shakespeare's *Hamlet*, Dostoyevsky's *The Possessed*, and Sophocles' *Antigone*) and by religious myths (Whiting's *The Devils, Pilate*). He focusses on individuals in extreme situations faced with a range of difficult choices (*A Generation, Ashes and Diamonds, Landscape after a Battle* and *Crime and Punishment*), but also deals with the psychological problems of ordinary people in everyday and trivial situations (*Two for the Seesaw, Birchwood, The Emigrants, Everything for Sale* and other contemporary films). There are enough issues here to absorb the creative energies of several different artists.

Even such a brief overview indicates that in some of their thematic areas Wajda's films and stage productions are complementary, that he uses his plays to tie up loose ends left in his films – and vice versa. The shift from one form of expression to another allows him to define his subjects more clearly and in greater depth. Examples that spring to mind are *The Wedding* or *The Danton Affair*, both of which Wajda attempted twice, first in a stage version and subsequently in a film adaptation. The thoughts he had accumulated on these themes in working through the stage productions could only be explored further by turning to a different medium. This variation in subject and form is an essential ingredient of Wajda's work. Although it explains why his films and plays have been criticized for their eclecticism, it is often forgotten that being 'true to oneself' purely in respect of form is easier than retaining the same truth in dealing fully with complex problems and issues. It is these issues that have marked out the points of intersection in the main themes of his films and plays from *A Generation* to *A Man of Iron* and from *A Hatful of Rain* to *Nastasya Filippovna* and *Antigone*.

Even though he can reach a wider audience through the screen, there are specific creative reasons that continually draw Wajda back to the stage. Theatrical production is a longer experience and the results are more profound. Filming, by its very nature, is technically complex, requiring the orchestration of large numbers of people, and it is expensive – all of which creates a pressure for quick artistic decisions. In the theatre there is time for discussion and a scene may be repeated, even re-shaped several times. Finally, there are opportunities for meditation, and its importance in Wajda's search for self-expression can be illustrated by an incident which occurred at the start of rehearsals for *The Idiot* at the Teatr Maly (Little Theatre) in Warsaw. We entered the theatre's superbly soundproofed rehearsal room. There was complete silence; Wajda listened for a moment, then said: 'Wouldn't it be good to isolate oneself completely, and just slowly work away here in this silence.' As he has repeatedly emphasized: 'What does the theatre have to offer me? – an intimacy, an immediate contact with my actors. Daily, we may confront each other, isolated, behind closed doors. The silence obtained in the seclusion of the rehearsal room is unique.'[2] However Wajda is more interested in conveying his message than in presentation. Since the idea is more important than the means chosen to express it, it follows that his choice of medium is secondary.

Wajda was trained as a painter, and his love of painting is evident, not only in his own intermittent scenography for the theatre and his art direction in his films, but also in the picturesque visuality of his work in general. Had Wajda continued as a painter he would probably be constantly changing his materials, shifting from oils to clay, from graphics to collage. The subject or theme dictates the choice of material and the form, while Wajda's recurrent concerns produce a basic link even though the materials differ and the style varies. Thus it is of secondary importance whether the work is sculptured in clay or marble, or performed on stage or screen. As the art theoretician Stefan Morawski states:

Wajda's artistic imagination is inborn and covers all aspects of art, and is also the basis for his ideas that do not pertain to art. His cinematic and visual conceptualization can be seen in his staging of *November Night*; while his theatrical and plastic visualization is apparent in his film *Pilate and Others*. *The Danton Affair* was an austere production, a courtroom drama with the accent placed on dramatic rhetoric. *The Promised Land* is full of motion, vivid and visually vibrating. This variety in his means of expression reflects both the range of Wajda's talent and the extensive use to which he puts his imagination.[3]

At the same time Wajda has focussed increasingly on a single art form. In the summer of 1972 he announced that he was leaving the film industry to devote himself entirely to work in the theatre, maybe even forming his own company. The reasons given were that he had exhausted the possibilities of cinema, and desired to exchange the mechanical way of portraying human relations on the screen for the more improvisational, fluid medium of live theatre. Subsequently he has put his cinematic talent to the service of the stage as in his 1977 documentary on Tadeusz Kantor's production of *The Dead Class* in the Cricot–2 Theatre. But it was politics that effectively enforced his withdrawal from film.

On 13 December 1981 martial law was declared in Poland. Wajda had sympathized with and been deeply involved in the Trade Union Movement, Solidarity. His film *Man of Iron* was an account of that movement, and he had participated in many of the cultural events associated with it. While martial law lasted he was not only attacked by the government and the official press. He was also forced to resign as president of the Polish Film Union and lost the directorship of the 'film unit' he led, which had not only been the vehicle for creating many of his own films but had launched numerous young directors. (The Polish film industry is divided into a number of separate units responsible for their own films under the leadership of eminent film directors.)

Since then it has been impossible for Wajda to work in Polish cinema, although *Danton*, a French film, was cast partly with Polish actors and

Introduction   11

received some financial backing from Poland. Wajda has therefore turned his full attention to the theatre, a more hermetical art form where political controversy is more easily accepted by the authorities. His most noted recent productions are the politically controversial *Antigone* and *Crime and Punishment*, the final play in his outstanding theatrical triptych based on the works of Dostoyevsky. Before the premiere of *Crime and Punishment* Wajda gave an extensive interview on West German television, which threw an interesting light on his new predicament, as well as on his attitude to theatre, film and his own career:

Q.: You are both a film and theatre director and you have often been asked about the relation of one art form to the other in your creative work. A few years ago you gave this reply: 'Film-making is my profession but I also need a hobby.' But currently in Poland you are working only in the theatre?

A.: I try never to mix the two. When I am working in the theatre, I look for the theatrical. For me a theatre is a convention, the relationship between the actors and a live audience. Cinema represents something entirely different. It is a photograph of life, a sort of imitation, the possibility to create something that gives us the impression of real life. When I work in the theatre I try to forget that I was ever a film director. I must admit though that after working in films for so long – and it must be all of thirty years – I sometimes need new inspiration and I find that, to a large extent, in the theatre. The fact that I am not making any films in Poland at present is not of my own choosing. This state of affairs was brought about by certain events. At the moment I do not envisage a film that I could make in Poland.[4]

Q.: You have made many films criticizing the current social situation in your country. The last two were *Man of Marble* and *Man of Iron*. By contrast, your theatre productions are based on the classics.

A.: That is true. My first films were political ones such as *Canal* and *Ashes and Diamonds*. These films had a specific function, and I must admit it would be difficult for me to back out from my political role in films. Cinema helps me perform a particular task. I want the country to submit to certain changes and films can decidedly help. They are very appropriate because, as a violent yet popular form of art, they can convey these ideas better than anything else. The theatre, on the other hand, runs along different lines. It benefits, and always will benefit, from its classical repertoire. Plays by Shakespeare, Chekhov, Sophocles and Schiller will always be performed. The problems covered by these plays are immortal. For instance, if one wanted to portray a cruel, tyrannical ruler, surely the best example that springs to mind would be *Richard the Third*. *Three Sisters* would be an obvious choice if one wanted to present the problems of existential futility. I think this classical repertoire gives us theatre directors fantastic material, which regenerates itself each time these problems are presented to a new audience.

Q.: In your production of *Antigone* only the text remained classical. By staging the play in this way what reaction did you wish to obtain from the audience?

A.: I think that no current play could portray the situation that arose in Poland three years ago better than the lines of Sophocles, written two thousand years earlier. To put it simply, there will always be a conflict between summary law, as represented by authority, and the law the people wish to follow: that age-old law, laid down by religion, agreed upon by us all. No other play describes this conflict better than *Antigone*.

It is worth noting that one of the main features of Wajda's attitude to the theatre, and particularly the classics in the theatre, becomes evident here. He displaces the classical story into a modern-day context, in particular selecting material for its relevance to the political situation in Poland today. For him the theatre is not only a place where artists may air their views, but where they should manifest their political standpoint.

Q.: Dostoyevsky holds a prominent position in your theatre work. You have staged *The Possessed, The Idiot*, and *Crime and Punishment*. What is it that draws you to this writer?
A.: Quite frankly, my loathing of him. I hate him and yet I admire his writing and his penetrating mind. Let's face it, it was Dostoyevsky who, in his novel *The Possessed*, uncovered what we now know as the terrorist movement. In *Crime and Punishment* he revealed that the world was heading in the worst possible direction. Crime would be tolerated, and a man may be murdered for purely theoretical reasons. These are all things that Dostoyevsky uncovered in the human soul. They horrify us but they exist and unfortunately have grown into a social disease. I also admire Dostoyevsky's method of writing. Although he never wrote anything in the form of a play, his books are wonderful theatrical material. He created his characters as one would make a collage. He collects certain features from people he has merely seen, or those he knew and combines them to make his characters extraordinarily vivid, full of contrast and contradictions. Thus Dostoyevsky had created drama few playwrights have achieved. Furthermore, we become acquainted with Dostoyevsky's protagonists through their dialogue. Dostoyevsky does not tell us anything about their 'inner selves', it is they who reveal themselves by constantly talking to one another, giving us a deep insight into them in the most objective way. This is also an important element of theatre.

At the same time I hate the man for his chauvinism, for his groundless opinion that Russia has something new to say to the world. That it is the Russian God who rules the universe, and that Russian Orthodoxy is the chosen religion. His religion. His airtight nationalism repels me, together with his hatred and contempt for the Poles, and the Germans and French also, come to that. For these reasons each new Dostoyevsky production causes me suffering, but then that is probably what keeps my relationship with him so alive.

Q.: I presume then that the works of Dostoyevsky have a contemporary, almost topical meaning for you.
A.: Yes, I think *Crime and Punishment* and *The Possessed* are especially pertinent. Dostoyevsky's novels are, as it were, illustrations of chosen fragments of the Gospel. The Gospel is the book of Christianity, the book of the West. I think that is one of the reasons why Dostoyevsky is more widely read, and better understood than other Russian writers, even though, in some ways, he is the most Russian. It is the influence of the Gospel on both these works that make them more European, easier for us to comprehend, and immortal.

Q.: May I ask you a few questions concerning your outlook on life? Are you religious? Do you consider hope an important principle in life? Do you believe in social progress?
A.: Along with the majority of the Polish intelligentsia, I have, as it were, returned to the bosom of the Catholic Church.

After the war, which seemed an incomprehensible absurdity and a contradiction of everything we had been brought up to believe, the Polish intelligentsia, especially artists and writers, tended to be strongly opposed to the Catholic Church. We no longer expected anything from it. However, what has taken place over the last thirty years has converted us to the belief that the Church is the guarantor of Polish national existence, and that this 'existence' may be protected most effectively by the Church. Yes, I support the Polish Catholic Church.

So far as hope is concerned, it is essential to us at present. 'Solidarity' was the 'new word' – as Dostoyevsky would put it – that was on everybody's lips during the last three years. I think that the political liquidation of Solidarity cannot change anything. It is of no consequence, because irrespective of the movement's fate, irrespective of its suppression, the significance of Solidarity is its spiritual content. In my opinion what occurred has immortalized the movement by transporting it into the realms of the ideal. There you have my outlook on the essential matter of hope.

As for the question of social progress, I think one cannot talk of social progress in a country that is not independent. A satellite country, a dependent society cannot form its own views and cannot be held responsible for them, since they are merely the outcome of necessity or chance. That is why, both in my films and other activities, I endeavour to widen the scope of liberty, so that people may express their real hopes and desires.

Q.: Finally, may I quote something rather negative that was said about you recently in a West German newspaper: 'Wajda is becoming a Euro-Director.' What does Poland mean to you? What significance does it hold in your thoughts, activities and work?

A.: Firstly, if I had wished to become a European director, I would have done so earlier, twenty-five years ago, at the start of my career. It was not for lack of opportunity that I stayed in Poland but because I believe that my place is there. Poland must be the base from which I work. I will go even further to say that only then can my work have any meaning. I am convinced that Poland will have something to say as regards today's world. Therefore it is important to me to be a director in Poland and to remain involved with that country.

What does Poland mean to me? Everything. My past and my future. It is the landscape that I see from my window, it is the nation's history and its art, past and future.

I want to take part in something vital. I have dreamt of this all my life; it is what I have always wanted. I have always believed that Poland occupied an important place on the European map and that Poland counts. Therefore, as a Pole, I am able to take part in significant and crucial events.[5]

This statement is not only the declaration of Andrzej Wajda's patriotism, it is also a vital component in his artistic philosophy. Although his presence is felt in world-wide culture, he remains primarily a Polish artist and it is his ties with Poland that give him his creative strength. In this way he may be likened to the Polish composer Chopin or the modern Polish poet Milosz. He finds much of his inspiration in Polish tradition, history and legend.

2   Stylistic experimentation: from *A Hatful of Rain* to *Play Strindberg*

Zygmunt Hübner, the artistic director of the Teatr Wybrzeze (Theatre at the Sea-side) in Gdansk, was responsible for drawing the young Wajda, already a well-known film director with successes such as *A Generation* and *Ashes and Diamonds* to his name, into the theatre. Today it is not unusual for a film director to work in the theatre, but in 1959 such a move provoked articles in the magazine *Film*, deliberating whether others would follow in Wajda's footsteps and the effect this would have on Polish culture.[1]

Wajda's choice of play, inspired by Hübner, was characteristic. The success of *A Hatful of Rain* in America was irrelevant, and the famous film by Fred Zinnemann based on it was unknown to him. As he remarked in an interview, 'if I had seen it, I would definitely not be able to free myself of its influence whilst working on the stage version'. The naturalistic trend in American drama, to which Michael Vincente Gazzo's play belonged, was not highly regarded in Poland at that time. Symbolist drama was in vogue, and the type of play that was popular ranged from Giraudoux to the Theatre of the Absurd. It was in conscious opposition to this that Wajda decided on Gazzo's realistic play, with its depiction of everyday life in minute detail.

On the surface *A Hatful of Rain* dealt with specifically American social problems. The main character, Johnny, is a veteran who returns from the Korean War as a drug addict. He becomes the victim of a gang of dealers. At first his middle-class family do not realize what is happening; later they are unable to help him. Only his brother wages a dramatic, yet futile, battle to save him. Johnny is killed when he cannot pay the dealers. However, the play has a deeper level than the obvious 'thriller' story-line. It shows the loneliness of one man in an uncaring society, the frailty of family ties, and the tragic consequences of war.

The play is sharp, even brutal, in its depiction of human character and human situations. Drugs and the settling of gangland scores have become clichés in contemporary American films, but at the time Gozzo's treatment of the subject was novel and might have appeared extreme to Polish audiences (creating problems of credibility for a director). Wajda accepted the principle of total naturalism on the stage, requiring that the wider, universal meaning of the play must not be hinted at by metaphor and symbolism, but must emerge naturally from the pictures of 'real life' created on the stage. However the set design incorporated metaphor in its background of the New York

Stylistic experimentation

1 *A Hatful of Rain*, Gdansk 1959. Johnny (Zbigniew Cybulski, centre) faces drug dealers.

skyline (a photomontage emphasizing the monotony of fire-escapes) that suggested the stifling effect of the urban world on the inhabitants of the apartment where the action takes place.

Due to the naturalistic need for 'truth', the actors' task was a difficult one. This was especially so, on a personal level, for Zbigniew Cybulski in the part of the drug addict Johnny. However, now at the height of his film career, Cybulski's brilliant portrayal of the tragic hero in the just-completed *Ashes and Diamonds* had created a new style of acting that had more in common with the American than the Polish School, and complemented Wajda's conception of the way the play should be acted. Wajda attempted to attain the same intensity of acting during rehearsals that can be achieved during each short 'take' in a film. At that time he was particularly fascinated with American cinema, especially the films of Elia Kazan and the actors he used, such as James Dean and Marlon Brando. He wanted to introduce the gut feeling and sense of reality that they displayed to stage acting, in sharp contrast to the formal, rhetorical and presentational acting that was still prevalent elsewhere in Poland.

The participation of the film star was one reason the show was so successful. Yet most of the critics reproached Cybulski for being too much himself and too hysterical. He was also accused of being repetitive and using gimmicks familiar to everyone from his previous roles. A review by Jerzy Bober was typical:

The play is too long and inconsistent and the actors' interpretation (especially Cybulski) seems arrogantly 'over the top'. Cybulski disenchanted me. His performance was too 'naturalistic' to be convincing. It seems that this talented film actor, dubbed the Polish James Dean, lost himself in the search for Art. His attempts to find a sub-text were forced and he fell into mannerism trying to attract the audience's attention. The director did not thwart him in this.[2]

For Wajda, however, this 'private acting' was a positive element precisely because it was so far removed from the traditional concept of 'theatre acting'. He negated conventional expectations and established new standards of realism. For instance, Cybulski so disliked the monotony of repeating the role each night that he played the part differently in each performance, often using his own words instead of the text. This not only called for extreme flexibility in his partners on stage; it challenged them to respond freshly to the dramatic situation, injecting an element of improvisation and immediacy that had a powerful effect on the audience. Recalling an occasion when Cybulski was late for the show, Wajda emphasized the value of his unpredictable behaviour in the production:

It was five minutes after the third bell. The audience was seated and waiting in silence. Suddenly a motor cycle drew up outside the theatre with a deafening roar. The hall doors, and seconds later. the auditorium doors crashed open. He appeared in his helmet, strode through the auditorium, and pushing the curtain aside, disappeared behind it. The curtain rose and he was already acting the first scene. There was no difference between him and the part he was playing. It was Johnny who had just arrived on his motorbike. The other actors took their cue from him and the show came to life.[3]

A Hatful of Rain was the most important production of the season. The play toured Poland, sweeping up enthusiastic reviews and creating long queues at the box-office. Its success was not only due to the popularity of the 'new stars', Wajda and Cybulski, but also because the subject of the play, and the way it was handled, were a revelation. As a leading critic commented:

Theatre has regained the potential it seemingly lost – one thought forever – in favour of films: the means of skilfully presenting life (as an equally accurate report of the truth) not in the form of a synthesis but in full detail; not in terms of platitudes, however, but

Stylistic experimentation

pathologically, with all the unexpected twists of the psyche. And this proposition was accepted with full-hearted rapture and breathless admiration by the audience... We were astonished by the combination of Gazzo's naturalism and Wajda's sharp, filmic realization.[4]

The years when the stage was reserved for the classics and non-controversial modern drama had created a craving: the need for a theatre depicting sharp conflicts and strong personalities, and this 'pathology' of which the critic speaks. The situation not only affected dramaturgy but also the technical side of theatre and the acting. Wajda had managed to assess the attitude of the audience correctly. In Polish theatrical circles at that time extreme realism — such as water flowing from a tap on stage — was no longer considered to be theatre. However Wajda wanted 'real water' to flow, in the sense of creating an 'imitation of life' where people's reactions and emotions would reproduce actuality. This new form of realism, which challenged established theatrical practice, and the controversial nature of the play's subject paralleled Wajda's films, which were equally novel in Polish cinema. The text of *A Hatful of Rain*, with its drug-addict veteran of the Korean War, might be American, but in this context the revolutionizing of technical approach and perspective acted as a catalyst for the Polish stage, just as works like *Ashes and Diamonds* created the Polish School of Film.

The undoubted success of his first theatrical venture emboldened the director to attempt a classic such as *Hamlet*. It is only now, in the perspective of time, that we can evaluate the line of thought Wajda decided to follow. Just as *A Hatful of Rain* relates to his own early films, his *Hamlet* is related to Polish literary tradition, where artistic creativity is subordinated to national history, in a way that was to become characteristic of his later work. The link to Polish culture here was provided by Wyspianski's essay *A Study of Hamlet*.

Stanislaw Wyspianski (1868–1907) was a great painter, poet and playwright. He was also a theoretician and producer of theatre. Influenced by European reformers like Richard Wagner and Gordon Craig, with whom he shared the vision of theatre as an autonomous art form, Wyspianski introduced a symbolist approach to theatre in Poland, which had a considerable effect on its growth in the twentieth century. In addition to his many plays, two of which (*The Wedding* and *November Night*) Wajda later directed, Wyspianski had written an essay analysing the different possibilities of staging Shakespearean tragedy. This reflected his theories on innovation in conjunction with the specifically Polish way of understanding history and tradition. Wyspianski's aim was to inject Polish traits into the mainstream of European culture. By basing his *Hamlet* on Wyspianski's suggestions Wajda wished, as it were, to achieve the process in reverse: to assimilate Shakespeare to the Polish stage with as many Polish characteristics as possible.

In his *A Study of Hamlet* Wyspianski not only gave his views on that particular play, but formulated his own theory on theatre and its place in society. One of the greatest Polish stage directors, Leon Schiller (1887–1954), has summed up these ideas in *The Mask*, edited by Gordon Craig, in the following way:

Thoroughly sifting the problem of Hamlet according to 'what there is in Poland for thought', he considers the problem of the production of Shakespeare 'and of that Shakespeare who wrote Hamlet' and sketches its picture, supporting himself on some historical data (to which, however, he attached no importance), and principally on the basis of the ideas expressed in 'Hamlet' which testify to its author as an ideal dramaturge, stage-manager and pedagogue of the theatre. Wyspianski dreams of that theatre 'whose end is to hold the mirror up to nature' and at whose head stands Shakespeare, ... Prospero 'whose charm is nothing else but intelligence', making servants of enemies, and humbling by its supremacy ... the true gift for divining people, ... the talent of people like Holbein, for instance, which knows how to 'read in the countenance of living people and to write it in a picture'.

He dreams of that theatre which, under the government of such an Intelligence, 'becomes a judgment hall where art, drama, artism, judge, and take also such a note, ... that as on a fishing-rod they bring conscience to the surface', he dreams of such an intelligent judgment 'inquiring into the conscience of the amphitheatre which,' however well it may mask itself, nevertheless 'will stammer out the truth at last wearied by the watchfulness of intelligence'.[5]

It is difficult to say how successful Wajda's production was in realizing these intentions. Wajda himself admits that when he began working on *Hamlet* he could not entirely rid himself of the limitations imposed by the 'traditional approach'. For instance he could not bring himself to cast Zbigniew Cybulski, the modern film actor, as the Danish Prince. He gave the part to Edmund Fetting who had also acted in *A Hatful of Rain*.

The influence of Wyspianski's *Study* was most obvious in the decor. The set matched, in almost every detail, Wyspianski's design based on medieval and Renaissance stage architecture. It formed a house-like structure on several levels, each comprising a number of 'cages', representing separate rooms: the Queen's bedroom, Polonius' apartment, etc. The proscenium reached far out into the auditorium bringing the actors closer to the audience – a commonplace occurrence today. In 1960, however, Hamlet delivering his famous speech 'To be or not to be' face to face with the first rows of the audience was considered a very daring step. Of course, this was far from being experimental. Although Wajda's Hamlet was speaking to the audience he did not cross the actual boundary that separated them. By contrast, barely two years later in similar adaptations of the classics such as *Kordian* and *The Tragic History of Doctor Faustus* (1963) Grotowski's '13th Row Theatre' confronted the audience directly and even mingled with it. Wyspianski had advocated abandoning traditional investigation into Hamlet's psyche and

Stylistic experimentation

2 *Hamlet*, Gdansk 1960. A general view of the set at the time of the play within the play. Hamlet (Edmund Fetting) and Ophelia (Elzbieta Kepinska) are seen far right.

that of the other characters as fruitless: 'It is solely THE EVOLUTION OF EVENTS that is interesting and worthy of any attention.'6 And this was the line Wajda followed, setting out the physical action clearly and allowing the audience to draw its own conclusions. The production consisted of sharply defined scenes, expressive theatrical effects and strong human characterizations. Wajda rejected the concept of Hamlet the idealist, wandering around the stage surrounded by a web of intrigue and surveillance, and Fetting played the role as a man of action. By moving the secondary characters further into the background he not only highlighted the main story-line of the play, but brought about a situation in which Hamlet was the mainspring of events, including the court intrigues.

To quote Konrad Eberhardt:

> On stage we found the same Wajda we know from the screen. Passionate, expressing his intellectual content by means of colliding contrasts. His actors produced a kind of 'convulsive' acting which is unafraid of being extreme or shocking. In this production darkness overcomes light, the helpless girlishness of Ophelia contrasts with the cruelty of Hamlet. Pangs of remorse cause the King to break down and sob loudly, and the murdered Polonius rends the arras with his head as he crashes to the ground. The moral paradoxes and conflicts are conveyed by acting that is far from genteel. It is disciplined but volcanic.[7]

In sharp contrast to most 'directorial theatre', Wajda avoided imposing any particular interpretation on the play – an early example of his characteristic respect for the text – though the way he jettisoned established traditions was typical. For instance, instead of the arrival of Fortinbras concluding the drama on an optimistic note, he gave Fortinbras and his soldiers the traits of brutal invaders. This, together with cutting of Fortinbras' final eulogy, cast a deeply pessimistic light on the action in retrospect.

There were flaws: an uneven cast, badly designed costumes which restricted the actors' movements and appeared extremely formal and conventional; and many critics complained that the pace was too slow. Despite the production's success and many positive reviews, Wajda was aware that his intention had not been fully realized. In retrospect he tended to blame his own inability to free himself completely from the fetters of conventional interpretations of the play and from the trap that the text sets for a director. As he commented with typical irony:

> I am convinced that *Hamlet* is a play impossible to direct. Although it is a work of genius, a masterpiece, the fact remains that it seems to be missing some pages. Quite simply, somebody copied it down incorrectly. Others of Shakespeare's plays may be better constructed, but this one, undoubtedly, is the most ingenious. Perhaps because it is as inconsistent as life itself. Since literature and art in general automatically strive for consistency, it is difficult to write an inconsistent play. The job of the director is to put the wonderful inconsistency and unpredictability of *Hamlet* into some form of order. That is the first step towards putting the play on at all. Although, trying to put that play into any sort of order, one runs the risk of involuntarily ruining it. I have yet to see anyone directing *Hamlet* inconsistently. For instance Ophelia could almost be two different people judging by her behaviour. The inconsistencies are always ironed out and so we are presented with 'a version' of *Hamlet* but never the play we envisaged when reading it.[8]

Even so, his own production deliberately reflected the inconsistencies he perceived in the text, and although this drew criticism from most of the reviews that noted it, at least one critic was sensitive to the potential value of such an approach:

> I think the director set about his production without having first found the key, and without giving it enough thought beforehand. I am not minimizing his labour or his intellectual sensitivity, on the contrary this shows a praiseworthy humility and artistic

Stylistic experimentation

responsibility. And, I think, a 'musicality'. Wajda knew he could not illustrate all that Shakespeare wrote. He wanted to explore how far he could go, whether the existing limitations could be overcome, and the play intensified by our dreams and reveries. That is why he made no cuts [sic]; he wanted to see whether the text stood up on its own, in spite of being aware that he was not totally in control, as other details were slipping through his fingers.⁹

When Wajda returned to the play, many years later in 1981, his approach was unchanged, though the circumstances were very different. Konrad Swinarski died suddenly in Damascus while rehearsals for his *Hamlet* were in progress at the Stary Teatr in Cracow, and Wajda was invited to take over the production. Although he used the same company, not wanting to copy his predecessor he recast the lead role. Swinarski's Hamlet was Jerzy Radziwilowicz, who had played the lead in Wajda's films *Man of Marble* and *Man of Iron*, and participated in many of Wajda's earlier plays. To underline the difference of his version, Wajda cast Jerzy Stuhr, a character actor who excelled at portraying ordinary, insignificant people in Polish films. Although enormously talented and expressive he neither behaved nor looked like the conventional image of the Shakespearean hero, so much so that his portrayal of the Prince was widely considered shocking. Stuhr's Hamlet was a modern intellectual, and at the same time an ordinary man with whom the audience could identify. As one Italian critic put it, he was 'the Prince from the street around the corner'.¹⁰ At the same time Wajda's staging formed an explicit contrast to this down-to-earth characterization.

Before the premiere, Wajda mounted selected scenes in the forecourt of the Wawel, the Renaissance Cracovian palace of the kings of Poland. Against the historical reality of this setting the fragments took on a monumental and static character, bringing to mind a *son et lumière* rather than a theatrical performance. In his first production in Gdansk Wajda achieved the effect of simultaneous action on stage with a multilevel set. At the Stary Teatr in Cracow the same purpose was served by having the stage divided vertically into two separate chambers where the action could also take place contemporaneously. For instance while Hamlet deliberated whether to kill Claudius in one room, the Queen was anxiously awaiting him in another. The two poles of this production, the monumental and the everyday, together with the experimental use of stage space, had already characterized Wajda's early work.

At the end of the fifties Gdansk was one of the most buoyant cultural centres in Poland. A large group of talented young actors, writers and directors gathered round the Teatr Wybrzeze and various local experimental student theatres. By the mid-sixties the focus had moved to Warsaw. So it was there in the Teatr Ateneum that Wajda commenced his rehearsals for

3   *Two for the Seesaw*, Warsaw 1960. Jerry (Zbigniew Cybulski) and Giselle (Elzbieta Kepinska): a rehearsal photo showing the intimate relation to the audience.

Gibson's *Two for the Seesaw* with two of his actors from Gdansk: Zbigniew Cybulski (Johnny Pope in *A Hatful of Rain*) and Elzbieta Kepinska (the Ophelia of his first *Hamlet*).

At Wajda's instigation a small stage was specially constructed at the Ateneum, which was particularly suited to a two-hander like *Two for the Seesaw* dealing with the psychological nuances of unrequited emotions. Named 'Stage 61', it was Poland's first theatre-in-the-round. A small stage, in an intimate auditorium, surrounded on all sides by the audience was a new experience for the director, actors and audience alike. But rather than

Stylistic experimentation

indicating a search for novelty, the concept came from Wajda's frustration at being unable to achieve the same focus in the theatre as on film:

> It annoyed me extremely that everyone saw the actor from a different view point... As a film-maker, used to the fact that the audience sees what I want them to see, I found it infuriating that someone sitting on one side would see everything against a different background to the person sitting on the other side. If that is how it must be, let them at least have freedom of choice. To me that seemed more truthful than leaving things to chance.[11]

In the case of *Two for the Seesaw* the round stage proved to be an exceptionally good idea. The setting called for in the text, representing the two separate apartments of Giselle and Jerry, joined only by telephone wire, was replaced by two adjacent settees. With this physical closeness the actors' hushed tones of insinuation graphically emphasized the theme of emotional inhibition. Cybulski's nervous, subdued acting, which had provoked criticism in other plays, was entirely appropriate for the character of Jerry, a man sensitive to the point of timidity. Kepinska was universally praised for the extreme subtlety in her psychological portrayal of Giselle. Since the staging of *Two for the Seesaw* did not involve much action, Wajda could concentrate on the characters and their 'inner life', which – as some critics pointed out – made the production seem exceptionally slow. However this was precisely Wajda's intention. For instance, he wanted the audience's entire attention to focus on the actors' faces as in a film close-up. In this the effect of the pacing was helped by strong lighting that picked out every detail of facial expression, and also by the fact that – due to the construction of the stage and the size of the auditorium – the audience could see the actors at very close range and only from the waist up. At least one reviewer was sensitive to Wajda's intentions, pointing out the parallel to the director's 1960 film about the psychological problems of modern youth:

> Wajda managed to extract a deeper meaning and discover a second layer of the play... His production of *Two for the Seesaw* was not only the psychological drama of two people but also an attempt to create the synthesis of the life of a human being, with only himself to rely on in a world of sharks, where none has time for anyone else. At first the fun Wajda had with the friendship developing between Giselle and Jerry was reminiscent of his film *Innocent Sorcerers*. Later, however, the play takes off on a more serious note and becomes really interesting, entering the sphere of true art.[12]

By contrast to the subtle nuances of *A Hatful of Rain*, Wajda's next production at the Ateneum strove for the monumental. Selecting a historical subject, John Whiting's *The Devils*, he conceived the scenes as a series of tableaux against the background of a massive and highly decorative baroque setting. The tableaux, everyone agreed, were very beautiful. As Andrzej Jarecki, one of the most respected Polish critics, wrote, 'Wajda fills the stage with interesting, vivid figures. The pictures that rise before our eyes involve us, even impassion us. They thrill us and sometimes even cause us to laugh, they absorb us.'[13] Yet Wajda himself considered the production unsuccessful, and almost every other element received harsh criticism. Indeed, the same review continued: 'but the meaning of the play, not easy to follow anyway, becomes muddled and is lost in the wealth of canvasses'.

Jarecki said delicately what other critics put rather bluntly. The central idea of the play had been sacrificed to visual effects. Furthermore, the mass hysteria of the nuns and its tragic effect on the priest Grandier were depicted in a simplistic and cartoon-like manner. Years later when Wajda talked about his production of *The Devils* (and the mistake he made therein), he described the staging as 'operatic'. He tried to achieve this effect of 'opera without music' by the actors' grand entrances, by orchestrating the tableaux like ensemble scenes, and by making the 'crowd' resemble the chorus in an opera. At the same time he attempted to play down the anti-Church theme, because he was aware of the strong religious feelings of the Polish audience: this however reduced dramatic content, depriving the play of its harsh and violent traits. The cast's lack of experience did not help matters either. Although on the one hand the characters were sketchy, their actions were presented so explicitly that the play lost all its metaphysical depth. This reflected the limited nature of Wajda's interpretation. In contrast to the drastic treatment of Ken Russell's film a decade later, which introduced a powerfully hypnotic note of real madness, Wajda portrayed the nuns' sexual-religious mania as a deliberate fraud from start to finish. Though clearly this rationalistic approach was intended to make the subject more accessible to his audience, the effect was to make the play – as critics unanimously agreed – 'trivial and boring'.[14]

Wajda's reaction to such bad notices was hardly surprising, given his own dissatisfaction with the production: 'That endeavour put me off theatre for a long time.'[15] However, before his seven-year retirement from the stage, in 1963 Wajda inaugurated a new era at the historical Stary Teatr in Cracow, re-opened under the artistic directorship of Zygmunt Hübner, the very man who originally had brought Wajda into the theatre. The production chosen for this occasion was Wyspianski's *The Wedding*, a play with strong cultural associations. Since its legendary premiere in 1901, this poetic drama has occupied a central position in the national repertoire. Even though it is produced each season in many theatres, its interpretation always varies, giving rise to endless discussion and disagreement. It is considered the most accurate portrayal of the 'Polish soul' and at the same time the sharpest attack upon it. It is a lofty poem and a biting satire, a cry of despair and a warning to Polish society. The action, inspired by a real-life event, is very intricate, full of

Stylistic experimentation

4   *The Devils*, Warsaw 1963. Mother Joan of the Angels (Aleksandra Slaska).

symbolism and references to Polish history and tradition. A poet, belonging to the gentry, has married a peasant girl, the fashion at the time. The wedding takes place in a country cottage. The guests represent a cross-section of society: intellectuals, artists, journalists, town folk and local peasants. Some of

5   *The Wedding*, Cracow 1963. The Host (Artur Mlodnicki) waves a sabre in patriotic enthusiasm.

the main characters are visited by apparitions. Wyspianski calls them *dramatis personae*. Characters from Polish history, literature and legend, they engage in a passionate dispute with the living about what it means to be Polish. Finally, the prophet Wernyhora rallies the oppressed nation to rebel in the name of freedom. The intellectuals, bourgeoisie and gentry are unable to take up this challenge. Despite the initial fervour of the peasants, the community is gradually overcome by apathy culminating in impotence. The play ends in a weird dance symbolizing the sleep-like paralysis of the nation and its inability to act.

The play is a challenge for directors and actors alike. It has a broad interpretative margin allowing it to be read in many ways: from the traditional to the topical. Since all educated Poles know the play (many of its lines are used in everyday speech) each new interpretation strikes a chord with the public. That year the tone had been set by an extremely popular production which had totally broken with tradition, turning Wyspianski's play into a kind of literary cabaret. In this context, Wajda's version seemed traditionalist and its innovative features were overlooked. However, its reception as a conventional interpretation was paradoxical. In staging *The Wedding* Wajda restricted his imagination in order to achieve scenic realism,

Stylistic experimentation

6   *The Wedding*, Cracow 1963. The Poet (Jerzy Nowak, to the right) sees the ghost of Hetman, the traitor (Jan Adamski) in his vision.

and although this was a completely new approach so far as that play was concerned, in corresponding to the stylistic standard established on the Polish stage by his previous work it appeared unexceptional. Indeed, the degree to which the production was accepted as 'normal' is a measure of its naturalistic conviction.

Where the treatment was traditional was in making loyalty to the author a predominant criterion. There were no cuts or changes in the text. The set was constructed according to Wyspianski's own design, and the action was presented in the era of the play's origin. The staging was realistic. The key to Wajda's interpretation was that the characters were actual people, not puppets in a national satire. Instead of being mere vehicles for conveying given ideas, the wedding guests, especially the intelligentsia, were outlined sharply and generically. Much care was taken with the psychological delineation of each character and its truthful expression. However, the tendency towards naturalism was bound to lead to a loss of poetry, and Wajda did not manage to find an adequate way of portraying the 'apparition scenes', nor the apparitions themselves. Critical opinion was sharply divided. Some appreciated the 'absence of modernizing apparatus and gimmicky ideas', praising Wajda for 'venturing beyond the dilemmas of current novelty-seekers'.[16] Others lamented that 'Nothing is left of *The Wedding's* great, almost mythomanical, bewitching, poetry. None of the theatrical magic remains. That is the price Wajda has paid for the radicalism and novelty of his interpretation.'[17]

In the light of Wajda's later film adaptation of the play (1972), alive with singing and dancing yet at the same time full of solemnity and bitter wisdom, it is obvious that the realistic emphasis did not represent his full vision of the text. Curbing his imagination was a way of mastering the material.

Seen in this context the theatre version in Cracow was a first attempt at meeting the challenge of a work that had always fascinated him. He admits, however, that without the experience of the stage version he would never have been able to make the film. In the theatre there was only a factual account of the play as written by Wyspianski; on film the same drama could be expressed in the form of a dream. With the help of close-ups, expressive camera work, editing and a variety of locations, he was able to combine the straightforward realism of *The Wedding* with its poetic vision, its counterpoint of irony and loftiness. Unrestricted by the pressure of theatrical tradition or the audience's reverential expectations for a national classic, he also managed to cross the seemingly insuperable barrier of airtight national traits and made the play accessible to non-Poles.

In the sixties Wajda's concept of theatre had not yet crystallized and he felt he had not yet tapped all the theatre's resources, nor capitalized on all its potential. While *A Hatful of Rain* and *Two for the Seesaw* were a revolt against conventional theatre, *Hamlet*, *The Devils* and *The Wedding* marked a return to it. He was at an impasse, unable to free himself from traditional definitions of theatricality, yet aware that he would not achieve the desired result by clinging to established formulas. His intention was to create a 'theatrical theatre'. However he was not yet resorting to innovatory techniques, but used the means available at that time within the existing framework and placed the greatest importance on the expression of the acting.

Retreating from the stage for the next seven seasons, he concentrated exclusively on films, amongst them the Napoleonic epic *Ashes* (1965), searching for his own personal mode of expression. In retrospect, those years were a time of reflection and deliberation on the theatre; a period preparing for a new phase of artistic work, in which he evolved his own dramatic

Stylistic experimentation

7 *The Wedding*, Cracow 1963. Bourgeois intellectuals being attacked by the peasants.

concepts and unique theatrical form. The first sign of this, in 1970, came with his production of *Play Strindberg*.

Apparently, on re-reading Strindberg's *Dance of Death* Friedrich Dürrenmatt came to the conclusion that 'This is an extremely good play, but very badly written!' And so he re-wrote it. The anecdote illustrates the very essence of the idea behind the pastiche entitled *Play Strindberg*. This playful instinct is the key to the correct interpretation of the play. In the process of stripping Strindberg of his metaphysics (parodied as 'plush and infinity') Dürrenmatt consciously put himself above the described events, as an author intellectually superior to his characters. This is bound to lead to irony and even satire. Yet he is not poking fun at Strindberg. Who or what, then, is the object of his satire? Is it the audience? Or maybe theatre itself?

Dürrenmatt took his characters and story-line from Strindberg – the dying husband, the disintegration of the family – then sharpened the situations and the dialogue. By bringing the 'inner life' of Strindberg's characters into the

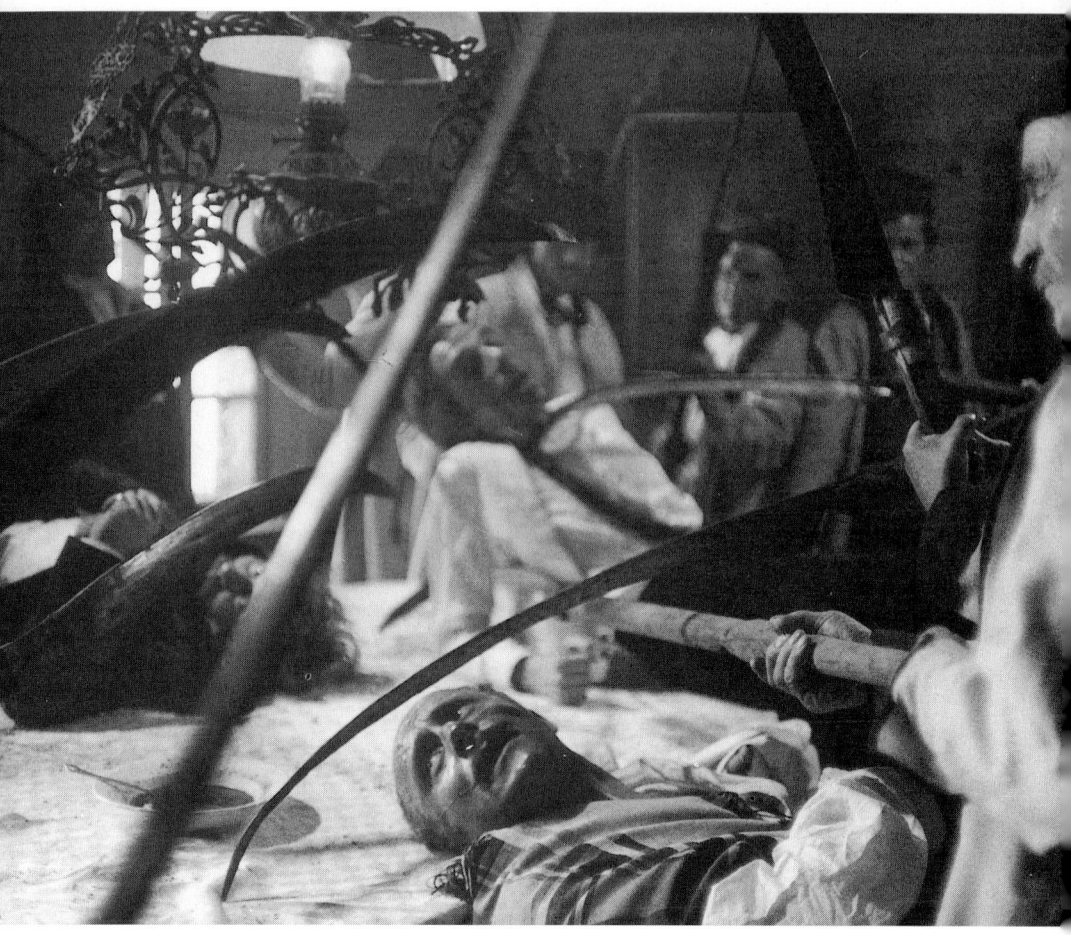

8 The same scene in the film version of *The Wedding* (1972).

open, he revealed it as exaggerated, providing comedy and at times tragic farce. Reality is transposed to a sphere of conventionality where the 'life and death conflict' of the original becomes merely a sporting contest, emphasized by the fact that the play is not divided into scenes but into rounds like a boxing match. For Wajda the fascination in this game of passion and perfidious pretence and the playing with words and feelings seems to have been the opportunity for creating uninhibited theatre out of nothing, for juggling around playfully with his own ideas. Since all is 'pretend', anything goes. Dürrenmatt makes fun of Strindberg. Why not make fun of Dürrenmatt? Especially since this funmaking is not as trivial as it may seem. It says something about transformations in human psychology, and the way the subject is treated by literature. (What for Strindberg seemed serious,

Stylistic experimentation

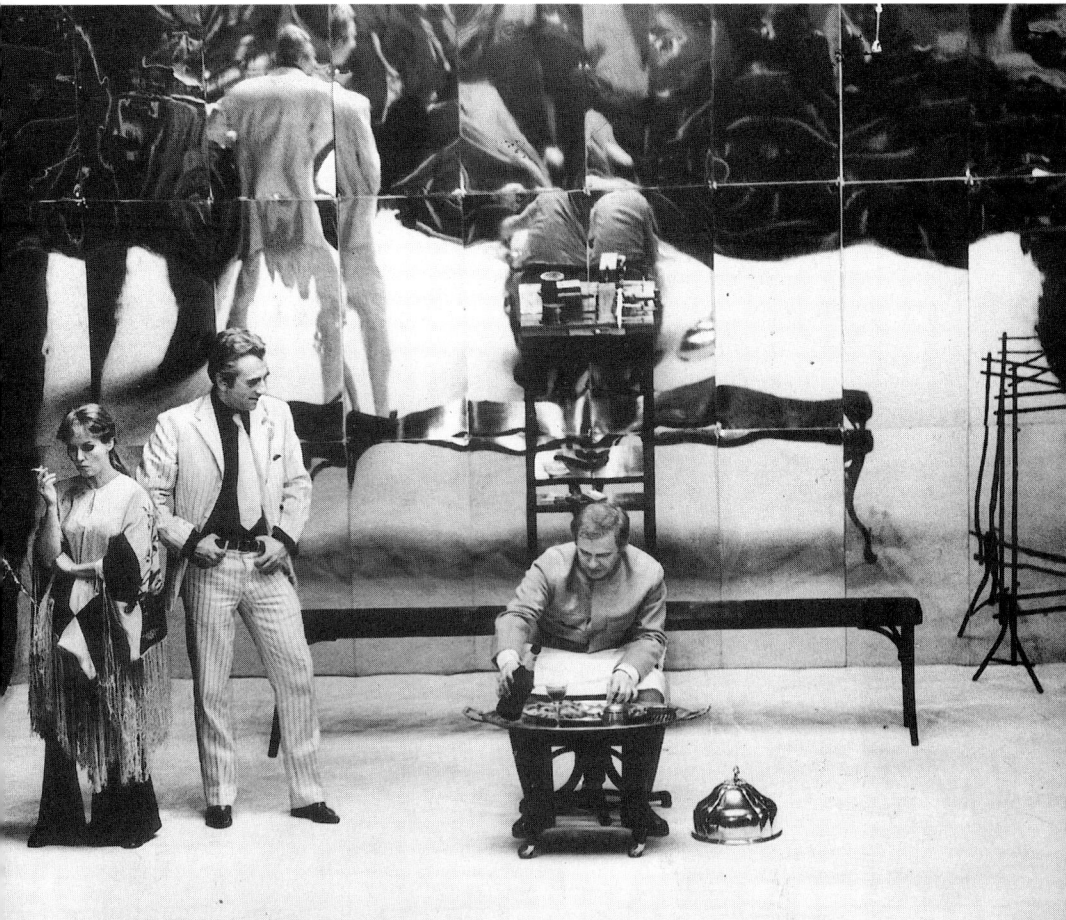

9 *Play Strindberg*, Warsaw 1970. Alice (Barbara Krafftowna), Kurt (Andrzej Lapicki) and Edgar (Tadeusz Lomnicki).

agonizing, mysterious can be a subject of irony and ridicule for modern writers.) Above all it casts an interesting light on the very essence of theatre. After all, theatre is a game for adults.

'So let's all have fun!' Wajda seems to exclaim as he directs *Play Strindberg*, unleashing a riot of imagination and giving his audience a foretaste of what is to come in his future productions. In some, such as *November Night* and *The Possessed*, his imagination might be restrained by literary demands, but in this case the play itself cried out for a 'no holds barred' approach. There was no idea, effect, device that was not suitable. Far from masking the playful side of theatre, every element of the production emphasized that nothing is anything but a game, a pretence.

Since the action is divided into rounds, a ring was constructed, and the type of bright floodlighting used at boxing matches installed. But who is going to fight in this ring? Is it just Alice, Edgar and Kurt? Wajda's answer was to place a huge mirrored panel along the back of the stage. As in the 'hall of mirrors' at the fun fair, the reflection of the audience in this mirror was blurred and warped. The effect was twofold: first it created an illusion that the ring was surrounded by spectators as in a real-life match. Secondly, on a symbolic level the characters in the play we were watching became a caricatured reflection of ourselves as we go about waging life's battles with deadly seriousness.

Stroboscopic light was used, together with a multitude of other lighting and sound effects. A gong sounded after each 'round' of conflict between the protagonists. Enlarged photographs were projected onto the screen as the family look through their photo album and music by Grieg was played. But the key interpretative element that tied these theatrical fireworks together was the style of acting which Wajda developed with his leading actor Tadeusz Lomnicki – the acting role as 'game playing'. According to Wajda: 'Lomnicki initiated me into theatre that lay beyond biological truth. A theatre of symbols and highly developed convention, at the same time far removed from conventional theatre. He acquainted me with ideas relating to form and a certain aspect of the theatre that had hitherto escaped my notice.'[18] The rapport between actor and director, so obvious in this production, was to become characteristic of Wajda's future productions.

As Edgar, Lomnicki transformed himself into a 'super-marionette', virtually reduced to a manoeuvrable part of the scenery, in a way that corresponded to the ideal of Edward Gordon Craig. There was no technical problem he could not overcome. This puppet, however, could also think, and Wajda made his display of skill yet another element in the game. Lomnicki performed mind-boggling tricks on stage. During his attack of amnesia his face became purple, then white as a sheet. He would hold his breath for an impossible length of time in order seconds later to bellow so loudly that it seemed he would tear his vocal cords. His body and voice became a virtuoso's instrument, underlining the artifice of performance and setting the tone, so that the other actors also became 'production elements'. In sharp contrast to Lomnicki, Andrzej Lapicki was reserved and calm in the role of Kurt. Lomnicki's performance was sensual – Lapicki's seemed to be an intellectual commentary. Barbara Krafftowna's Alice was not just an onlooker, nor merely the cause of the conflict between the two men. She communicated perverse pleasure in watching them fight and leading them on. She displayed the destructive strength of a woman who enjoys driving men to despair. Their skills augmented the rich mosaic which Wajda had

Stylistic experimentation

10   *Play Strindberg*, Warsaw 1970. General view of the set.

composed using all possible theatrical resources. However the 'pure form' (the acting of Tadeusz Lomnicki) was employed thematically. In the same way that the text of *Play Strindberg* presents a game played out against the backcloth of the deep psychological analysis of *The Dance of Death*, so the acting was not just pure showmanship but each of the performances also possessed a psychological depth. Indeed, the farcical exaggeration itself served as an insight into the darkness of the human soul.

This intelligent theatrical game, so brilliantly presented, was not only an inspiration but also a lesson that revolutionized Wajda's understanding of stage acting and its function in a production. It formed the preface to a new chapter in Wajda's theatrical career, a fruitful period that was to yield a harvest of works of importance and world-wide acclaim.

3 Andrzej Wajda's 'total theatre': *The Possessed, November Night* and *The Danton Affair*

Working on *Play Strindberg* was a turning point in Wajda's theatrical career. The conclusions he had reached in that production were the starting point for *The Possessed*, and later *November Night*. At a glance this may seem paradoxical, as Dürrenmatt's drama is basically 'a chamber piece', whilst these are monumental works requiring epic staging. The prospect of putting an overwhelming novel in its entirety into a visual and scenic context was daunting. However, the multiplicity of possibilities that Wajda had discovered in staging *Play Strinberg* offered potential solutions.

In deciding to confront one of the mightiest works ever written about the human soul, *The Possessed* (in Polish *The Devils*) by Fyodor Dostoyevsky, Wajda did not even attempt to convince his actors that the assignment they were jointly undertaking had any chance of success. According to him the atmosphere in the Stary Teatr was one of uncertainty and apprehension.

Work started on the stage adaptation by Albert Camus. But although Camus was credited on the Cracow posters very little of his adaptation remained in the actual structure of the production. In arriving at the eventual script Wajda held Dostoyevsky's novel in one hand and Camus' play in the other. He treated both equally but in moments of doubt he always referred to Dostoyevsky's novel, that is, to the novel as read, understood and envisaged by him, Andrzej Wajda, 'envisaged' probably being the operative word.

> Out of the twenty-four scenes in Camus' adaptation, only four to five scenes were retained in my production. The remaining scenes were simply taken from the novel itself. I shall try to explain why: Camus had written his version for specific actors at a specific theatre in Paris. Besides, he was led astray by one simple fact. Since much of the action takes place in Barbara Pietrovna's salon, he treated *The Possessed* as 'drawing-room drama'. But let's face it, that was a totally misguided interpretation. I began to work on the play from Camus' text but I found too much was missing. He had omitted the fragments I thought most important; scenes I particularly remembered from the novel had been left out. I delved into the pages of the book to find them. I began 'writing' the play in the course of rehearsals, just as Camus had done. Two brilliant young actors portrayed Stavrogin and the young Verkhovensky, so I naturally gave them the bulk of the text, in the same way as Camus had written his play for Blanchard and Balashova. I could not present a Polish audience with Camus' adaptation; I felt it would not fascinate them. After all, our knowledge of Russia is deeper and more precise.
>
> (Excerpt from Andrzej Wajda's speech at a symposium on Dostoyevsky at the Polish Academy of Sciences)

Andrzej Wajda's 'total theatre'

11 *The Possessed*, Cracow 1971. Piotr Verkhovensky (Wojciech Pszoniak) and Nikolai Stavrogin (Jan Nowicki).

In 'envisaging' *The Possessed*, Wajda's highly imaginative three-dimensional realization of the setting was of prime importance and shaped all other components. The bare stage was covered in sticky mud (like that of the Steppes) right up to the horizon – from which, in turn, rose a leaden sky permanently obscured by cloud, forming a bleak background which emphasized the boundlessness of the Russian landscape. Alternating pieces of furniture placed in the mud symbolized various interiors. The mud stuck to the hems of the actors' garments. It was primarily this design that helped to transport the action from the pages of the novel to scenic reality and created the atmosphere of the production.

Even the very beginning of the play was characteristically strange, opening with Camus' ending. Seated on a small chair on the proscenium, Stavrogin makes his confession. From time to time he shields his eyes from the shaft of light projected onto him. The first words he utters, 'I Nikolai Stavrogin . . .', give a premonition of the extraordinary nature of his confession. He shudders feverishly, beads of perspiration appear on his forehead. He speaks fast, nervously, almost choking on his words; his eyes are wild with an inhuman fear. Somewhere nearby the clicking of a typewriter can be heard; it stops whenever he stops speaking. One begins to wonder if this is not an interrogation. As Stavrogin starts to speak of the murder, the

12 *The Possessed*, Cracow 1971. Stavrogin's confession (Stavrogin: Jan Nowicki). Matriocha, the girl he raped, is seen in the window.

little girl he has violated, or rather her ghost, appears. She stands, deathly white, on a little balcony to the right of the stage, clutching her doll in her arms. It is still difficult to grasp fully what is going on. Not until the monk Tichon enters does it become clear that this is a confession. The appearance of the monk has a soothing effect on Stavrogin, who seems to compose himself as he speaks to his confessor. His composure is only momentary, however, for he suddenly leaps up and bites the astonished priest's ear with all his might, then falls to the ground in convulsions. An unearthly shriek rends the air, followed by shouts and groans. Stavrogin's prostrate figure is encircled by dark, shapeless, faceless forms, carrying rattles. They seem to be whispering, uttering incomprehensible words. When the shadowy figures disperse, the stage is empty.

Now the action can start; a narrator is used, as in Camus' version. The narrator is also perspiring heavily, there is fear in his eyes too and he speaks his lines curiously; very fast, nervously, rubbing his hands. This feverish atmosphere begins to affect the audience; we are seized by a premonition of evil. We cannot rid our ears of that inhuman shriek, the whisperings, the unintelligible words and snatches of songs. The impersonal black shapes (who later bring on the props and perform the set changes) are chillingly menacing in their enigmatic silence. It is not difficult to deduce where Wajda got the idea of those black figures: he had seen them in the Japanese *Bunraku* puppet theatre, where they are called *Croco*.

The continual presence of those gloomy observers/stage-hands can be interpreted in different ways. From one perspective they personify 'The Devils' of the Polish title, although the director considered this too narrow and simplistic. In his concept it is the characters themselves who become 'The Devils':

Now there happened to be a large herd of pigs feeding on the hill-side, and the spirits begged him, 'Send us among the pigs and let us go into them.' He gave them leave; and the unclean spirits came out and went into the pigs; and the herd, of about two thousand, rushed over the edge into the lake and were drowned.

The men in charge of them took to their heels and carried the news to the town and country-side; and the people came out to see what had happened. They came to Jesus and saw the madman who had been possessed by the legion of devils, sitting there clothed and in his right mind; and they were afraid.   (*New English Bible*, Mark 5: 11–16)

Such is the motto of Dostoyevsky's novel and it was this frenzied rush to the very edge of the precipice that Wajda showed in his production. His protagonists were people possessed by 'evil forces', unable to comprehend the world or themselves, tearing blindly towards their own destruction, terrified but unable to stop. Hence the pace of the production continually gathered momentum, the tempo became breathless and frenzied. This was not achieved by sound effects or fast montage alone, but by the style of acting: particularly that displayed by Wojciech Pszoniak in the part of Verkhovensky and Jan Nowicki as Stavrogin. The former presented an agitated and verbose 'devil'. His movements across the stage were angular and frenetic – strange leaps, trotting instead of walking. Words poured from him furiously until he was forced to stop for breath. Nowicki was the opposite, and also quite different from when we first saw him in the 'confession scene'. He was embodiment of supremely controlled and ironical evil. His face showed utter contempt and a permanent smile played upon his lips; in his eyes, however, there lingered immense sadness. There was an unforgettable moment when Stavrogin turns upstage after refusing to collaborate with 'the group' and Verkhovensky chases after him in desperation. Pszoniak, his hair streaming, his arms flailing like some crazed windmill, skips after the disappearing figure. Despite the restrictions imposed by space, the scene seemed to go on and on until the actors virtually melted into the horizon.

Each scene was followed by a blackout and piercing music, and the lighting played a very important part, both in evoking the specific atmosphere of each episode and in creating an illusion that the action was taking place in many different settings. For example, in the scene depicting the meeting of Verkhovensky and the conspirators a lamp hung low over the table at which they were sitting. Billows of smoke from their cigarettes swirled in its light, creating an atmosphere of conspiratorial intimacy although in actuality the scene took place in the middle of a huge empty stage. The screens brought on by the *Croco* also helped to create an intimate atmosphere, making the spectator feel he was watching the action in close-up. This was particularly true for the scene in which Maria Shatov gives birth to her child. At the other extreme, the illusion of a huge expanse of space, suggesting the Russian steppes, was created by placing the action at the very back of the stage, against the 'horizon'. This was especially effective in Stepan Verkhovensky's death scene: the old man lay on the ground covered by a sheepskin coat, with his loyal friend Barbara Pietrovna seated beside him reading the Bible. Behind them, at the very back of the stage, stood the coach in which the old philosopher had wanted to escape. They were not alone however: an immobile, black figure held the reins in readiness, waiting for the soul that was soon to depart the man's body. Purely technical devices added to the 'totality' of this theatrical event, one of the most striking effects being the flickering lamp used to light the stage during the decisive dialogue between Kirylov and Verkhovensky. (Kirylov is totally disillusioned with life. He sees suicide as the ultimate freedom for man. Verkhovensky chooses him to be one of his organization's martyrs, since he seems to be quite prepared for death.) This electric lamp was wired to a hidden microphone with a device regulating the strength of light according to the volume of sound. Thus when Kirylov whispered, the light would dim; when Verkhovensky shouted, the lamp would glare brightly. This effect, combined with the superb acting, created an extraordinary atmosphere. When the light was dim, the faces of

13 *The Possessed*, Cracow 1971. Death of Stepan Trofimovich Verkhovensky (Wiktor Sadecki, centre). He is accompanied by Barbara Pietrovna (Zofia Niwinska).

the two men were obscured, then suddenly as the light flared up, the audience caught sight of their grimacing features, twisted with fear, pain and cruelty. The climax of the scene comes when Verkhovensky, with kicks and blows, forces Kirylov to commit suicide. The latter suddenly ceases to represent the

14 *The Possessed*, Cracow 1971. Piotr Verkhovensky (Wojciech Pszoniak, on the right) forces Kirilov (Andrzej Kozak) to commit suicide, as the 'dark ones' wait in the background.

epitome of ultimate freedom and instead becomes an absurd, sacrificial victim on the altar of evil and baseness. After Verkhovensky has forced a revolver on the protesting Kirylov, the flash of a gunshot lights the stage one last time and the triumphant 'devil' runs off with a diabolical scream.

The extraordinary atmosphere achieved in this scene was heightened by all available means. The technical effects and the tension created by the acting were woven together so subtly that if a single one were removed, the entire tension would collapse. This illustrates one of the basic traits of Wajda's 'total theatre'.[1] Having amassed all his effects, he weaves a sort of net of dependence: the directorial concepts on their own may not mean much, they may even be slightly suspect, but when blended into the production, each falls into place, and together they generate an extraordinary emotional intensity. To achieve this everything is sacrificed: realism, even thematic consistency — as the famous final scene of *The Possessed* illustrates. The hooded figures, who until this moment had only been observers and helpers carrying out the functions of stage-hands, suddenly assume a dominant role in the action, interfering cruelly and relentlessly in the destiny of the protagonists. They accelerate the oncoming catastrophe, pushing the unfortunates towards the chasm. As Stavrogin disappears behind the door in the centre of the stage, the 'dark ones' slowly prepare the noose before following him. The methodical way they perform their task contains a menace which is an augury of the inevitable tragic finale. Then follows the reading of Stavrogin's final letter in Barbara Pietrovna's drawing-room. In his letter Stavrogin urges Dasha Shatov to join him in Switzerland; Dasha, suspecting nothing, moves calmly and slowly towards the door but before she grasps the handle, the door swings open and a final hideous cry fills the air. Behind the door — as described in Dostoyevsky's novel — hangs Nikolai Stavrogin. Surrounding the swinging body stand the dark helpers, gloating. The source of the cry is left unclear. It might have been Dasha's as she made the gruesome discovery, or the triumphant shout of the devils, their evil work reaching its climax. In either case the impression contradicted Wajda's intentions by specifically pointing to these hooded figures as the personification of 'The Devils' referred to in the title. The actual significance of the scene, however, was clearly of secondary importance to Wajda compared to its emotional strength. It was an indisputably powerful way to end an extraordinary play.

I remember to this day the first impact of Wajda's production and the magnetic influence it exerted upon me. And although I watched it many times subsequently, I never managed to free myself from its stifling atmosphere. The virtuosity of the actors, and the artistry of the director, combined with an undefinable, but ever-present sensation that one was being initiated into the very depths of human experience.

This atmosphere grew out of the rehearsal process, and Wajda's working technique, based largely on improvisation, was specifically designed to foster it. He would place his actors in unexpected, extreme situations in order to produce the emotional tension required. This was exacerbated by the degree of uncertainty about the theatrical success of the venture that he projected, as he emphasized in an interview about the realization of *The Possessed* in the magazine *Teatr*:

> I would like to return to my starting point, to that feeling of inability that filled me at the time. During the three months of rehearsals I tried to infect my actors with the same feeling, and finally succeeded. This was not perversity. I was trying to avoid cheating myself, as a child does when it closes its eyes and thinks no one can see it. I knew that my production could not parallel Dostoyevsky's masterpiece. I merely managed to grasp its shadow. Maybe it was a lucky shadow, the best there is, but even now I do not think of it in any other way, although I consider it to be my most 'complete' realization in the theatre.
>
> The actors believed they were taking part in something that was doomed to fail. The dress rehearsal did not take place at all because within the first ten minutes [of the run-through], one of the actors, Kazimierz Fabisak, died on stage. So the actors did not perform in front of any sort of audience until the first night. Right up to the very end, they were entirely in my hands; I was the sole witness of their struggle with Dostoyevsky and their only judge. I encouraged them, but at the same time gave them no hope that they might win. So much so that we wondered whether to insert an entr'acte, fearing that during the interval we might lose most of our audience. At the premiere when the audience started applauding, the actors were so astonished, they stopped acting. There was a long pause; they did not know what to make of the audience's enthusiastic reception. I consider that to be my greatest directorial feat. Despite the fact that I gave my actors no confidence during the three months of rehearsal, they would not give up. There was something kamikaze in this. After watching the show, Konrad Swinarski asked me how I managed to produce such fear in my actors' eyes. I considered that 'fear' to be my greatest accomplishment.[2]

Wajda calls his production of *The Possessed* his 'greatest theatrical adventure'. It was also an eruption – perhaps only partly conscious – of a certain poetry and style that characterizes his brand of 'total theatre'. It was the culmination of the laborious exploration of theatre that marked his early work, and it followed Dostoyevsky's own prescription for a dramatization of his novel: 'There is some secret in art which causes the epic form never to find its equivalent in the dramatic form. On the other hand, adapting the novel drastically, would be quite another matter . . . retaining only an episode, or otherwise taking the main theme but entirely changing the subject matter.'[3]

This technique for translating the spirit of a novel to the stage was used again – many year later – in Wajda's *Nastasya Filippovna*, based on *The Idiot*. More directly, however, the experience of atmospheric, emotional involvement gained in *The Possessed* led to his next production at the Stary Teatr, *November Night*, in which his 'total theatre' style reached its peak and was carried through to its final conclusion.

November Night, another of Stanislaw Wyspianski's plays in the standard Polish repertoire, is not an allegorical satire on society. It is a monumental work based on the 1830 Uprising against Russia, which not only portrays historical events, but interprets them poetically and philosophically. The

15 *The Possessed*, (new version), Cracow 1984. Meeting of the revolutionaries. Stavrogin (Jan Nowicki) is seated third from the left, and Verkhovensky (Jerzy Stuhr) first on the left.

action takes place on the night of 29 November 1830, when a handful of young Poles stirred up a national rebellion against the might of Russia. In addition to the Polish insurgents, the protagonists include the Grand Duke Constantine, brother of the Czar and Commander of the Polish army, and his Polish wife Joanna Grudzinska. However, Wyspianski also introduces ancient gods, who stand in judgement over events, his idea being that since history is forged in the domain of the spirit and people's actions are determined by fate, this can be personified by mythological characters steering the destiny of nations. Wyspianski also includes dream sequences to project the characters' thoughts and longings. In these scenes the world of gods and men are interwoven: Constantine can become Ares the god of war, appearing in Warsaw as he would beneath the ramparts of Troy.

Such contrasting levels of action make *November Night* a very difficult play to produce in the theatre. Its complex mythological symbolism cannot always be easily understood by a modern audience. Its form is inconsistent, closer to that of a poem than a play; some fragments are not as well written as others, making some sequences sound old-fashioned or unintentionally humorous. The first task for any director is therefore to find a uniform overall style to cover up the play's formlessness and modify the occasionally turgid passages.

Wajda's initial decision – characteristically simple and seeming obvious in hindsight – was that the mythological scenes should be sung. This idea was later developed to embrace other scenes, with music written by the composer Zygmunt Konieczny, who had worked with Wajda on *The Possessed*, until *November Night* became something resembling opera. Thanks to the brilliant atmospheric score, that served as an emotional intensifier, the mythological sequences ceased to be lectures on the philosophy of history and began to exert significant imaginative appeal. This was reinforced by the suggestive simplicity of the set design, which allowed the audience to fit in details from their own experience.

On either side of the stage, the famous statue of the Polish King Jan Sobieski and branches of trees represented the Lazienki Park of Warsaw, providing a minimal outline for the scene of most of the action: the Belvedere Palace, residence of the Grand Duke. The rear of the stage was encircled by plain walls. The scene-changes were achieved very simply; by a lighting change, or the placing of a piece of furniture on this almost bare stage. Yet the succession of scenes was so varied that the audience were tricked into believing that the set was gorgeously extravagant. One scene followed another swiftly, with a black curtain being drawn across the stage to create sharp transitions in a technique reminiscent of film editing.

A sung prologue set the tone for the production and provided the audience with a key to the interpretation of the play. A metaphorical augury of coming events, it was filled with extraordinary pathos – due mainly to the poignancy of the music – and led into a rendition of Wyspianski's own stage directions (describing the Cadet School corridor where the historical insurgents gathered before the 1830 Uprising), set to music and sung very softly by a hidden choir. The set, gradually coming into focus, was realized exactly in accordance with the author's instructions. Right up-stage was a door, which was made to look diminutive against the empty expanse of the unlit acting area. As the chanted evocation of the scene died away Jerzy Stuhr in the role of the leader of the Uprising, an officer named Wysocki, dashed onto the stage and with one sharp movement flung open the double doors to reveal a brightly lit classroom, crammed with cadets seated at their desks and standing out in striking chiaroscuro against the blackness of the rest of the stage. Wajda treated the word 'school' literally, casting juvenile actors as the cadets so that their immature adolescence emphasized the theme of youthful heroism. Wysocki began his long monologue as he stood in the doorway. The musical accompaniment transformed it into aria, a clarion-call to arms, to which the cadets responded eagerly, throwing on their overcoats, slinging ammunition pouches over their shoulders. As the arms were distributed the stage was filled with boys in uniform in a sequence reminiscent of army drill, which yet contained a foreboding of a last farewell. To the urgent beat of a drum, the cadets led by Wysocki began to march towards the audience.

The pathos of the opening, heightened and given concrete form in this scene, was maintained throughout. But the danger of emotional saturation was offset by the clarity and rigour of Wajda's interpretation. As the action developed, the intellectual propositions contained in the play were brought out, particularly in the scenes between the Grand Duke and his wife; while the youth and naivety of the cadets personified not only this particular uprising but stood as a metaphor for all national insurrections which, born of the noblest and purest of intentions, are still condemned to an agonizing confrontation with the reality of power politics and historical inevitability. In *Ashes and Diamonds* Wajda had portrayed the tragic generation of the Second World War through the ascetic medium of film. This time he portrayed the lost generation of 1830, making use of the whole range of possibilities open to the stage and 'operatic' music. But the underlying tragedy remains the same, and the enthralling visual effects, the sheer theatricality was no less important than the historical meaning and the patriotic significance. In sharp contrast to the popular appeal of the rebels' idealism, the scenes concerning the Grand Duke were highly controversial.

In Polish literature the Grand Duke epitomises the rapacious grip of Russian oppression, *Kordian* by Juliusz Slowacki being the best-known example. Wajda's interpretation explicitly broke with this deep-rooted tradition in Polish historiography and literature. Instead of a historical stereotype, in this production Constantine was portrayed as a man with a complex personality, and his inner conflict was brilliantly conveyed by Jan Nowicki. Torn between his loyalty and sense of duty to his brother the Czar, and his secret wish to take the throne of an independent Poland, attached to all things Polish by his passionate, if crude, love for his Polish wife, he nevertheless hated this 'nation of rebels'. He could be tyrannical and cruel; seconds later he would be tapping at his wife's bedroom door begging for her favours. He made use of informers whom he in turn despised. He accepted the allegiance of Polish traitors while exhibiting his contempt for them.

An equivalent broadening of historical outlook and challenging of conventional stereotypes was evident in the characterization of Joanna Grudzinska. The actress Teresa Budzisz-Krzyzanowska portrayed her as a woman deeply torn between her commitment to a national cause and love for

16 *November Night*, Cracow 1974. Pallas Athene (Barbara Bosak) leads cadets to the attack; Jerzy Stuhr (as Lieutenant Wysocki) with the sabre.

her husband, who by a decree of fate, stood at the head of enemy ranks. Of her own dilemma Joanna says: 'A husband and brother must fight against each other.' Wajda placed a strong accent on the sensual side of Constantine's and Joanna's relationship; they were sexually dependent on one another. It is irrelevant that this interpretation — although based on indications in the text — might not be strictly historically correct. It served to sharpen the psychological aspects of the characters in depicting Joanna as a deeply unhappy woman, tragically in love. Their intimate scenes showed two people entangled in a sado-masochistic union, cast upon the turbulent sea of history, with their tainted love and disenchantment.

Given this depth of characterization it would have been a natural temptation to portray Constantine as a tragic hero. Instead, in key scenes he was presented as almost a grotesque figure. During fits of terror he did not recognize his own servants, who had to dress him as one would a child. The 'history book' concept of Constantine was done away with, and he received the features of a fully psychologically delineated stage character.

Wajda not only successfully presented the 'two domains' that Wyspianski wrote about: the diverse worlds of gods and man. He also exposed their inner relationship. Myth and reality, suffering and sublimity, courage and baseness intermingled in the whirlpool of history. The way this was managed is best illustrated in the treatment of a poetic scene entitled 'The Farewell of Ceres and Persephone'. The two ancient goddesses, mother and daughter, appear in the ranks of the 'young heroes'. One of the youthful rebels approaches Persephone, plucks a sheaf of corn from the bunch of wheat and wild flowers she is carrying, and proceeds to eat the seeds. This small gesture symbolizes the way the worlds interpenetrate. The world of myth, legend and rousing hymns casts a shadow upon those doomed to live in the human — yet often inhumane — world, initiating their tragic actions.

After bidding farewell to her mother, Persephone slowly sank into a chasm of blazing light. During the dream scene in the second act, it was from this same opening that Joanna appeared. This atmospheric, mysterious sequence shifted the perspective on the two worlds: fable merged with psychology, archetype with motivation. Constantine, as Ares, rose from the swirling smoke surrounded by goddesses. The real Joanna stood by the proscenium. As she dreamed, her other self appeared behind her and embraced the triumphant god of war. Splitting the characters in this way not only exposed the myth/man connection beneath the apparent moral opposition established in the text. It also emphasized Joanna's psychological conflict. The baroque wealth of Wajda's imagination evolved naturally from a consistent reading of the play, and this counterpoint between symbol and actuality reflected the fundamental structuring principle of his production. Visual parallels were established between widely separated scenes, patterns of blocking recurred, thematic motifs were restated throughout the action. Charon's boat moves out from the smoke-filled depth of the stage, and the dead arise to disappear forever into the gulf of eternity, Poles and Russians,

17 *November Night*, Cracow 1974.

traitors and heroes alike. This scene finds its 'counterpoint' in the penultimate scene: Walerian Lukasinski, one of Poland's political martyrs who spent most of his life imprisoned in Russia, was given lines from the *Ode to Youth* by Adam Mickiewicz to sing: 'Hail, hail thou dawn of man's new liberty! Salvation's sunrise will disperse the night' – words of hope known to every Pole. Only in death do enemies become united and can legends make heroes out of traitors. In context this emphasis was shocking: a radical rewriting of history which gave equally human features to the brother of the Czar who had guarded the interests of Imperial Russia and to the Polish patriots, whose destiny it was to fight for freedom, and who spent years of hell in Siberia or exile.

Some critics found the conglomeration of effects 'gimmicky'. Others thought his 'style' over-illustrative, that it elaborated on expressive features excessively and necessarily led to tautology. Although *November Night* was among the most visual of Wajda's productions, however, the imaginative development of all the machinery of theatre in it was subordinated to the radically new, indseed bitter interpretation of an accepted classic, the challenging of convention and cliché that is characteristic of his creativity.

The force of Wajda's production lay in the way it balanced emotional evocation against intellectual debate on historical fact, portraying a crushing defeat while reaffirming hope. As the critic Marta Fik has pointed out: 'Wyspianski's patriotism seems naive today. In the Cracow production that naivety was not only noticeable, it was emphasized, but not without specific purpose. Wajda's heroes are not necessarily positive. The events of that November night are not supposed to be a challenge but a warning against the dangers of exalting certain myths, and the self-assurance of "impartiality".'[4]

Wajda's 'style' is primarily characterized by his ability to create hugely expressive 'pictures' composed of all those elements present at a given moment, on the stage or screen. Two important components of these tableaux are the intensity of the acting and the strong accent placed on sound (music and song in *November Night*, screams and murmurings in *The Possessed*). Supplemented by the careful positioning of figures, evocative stage properties and atmospheric lighting they present powerful images of great beauty. Since the action is divided into short sequences, these nodal points follow in swift succession, making use of all possible theatrical devices to 'attack' the spectators on all sides, subjecting them to a wealth of intense and highly emotional experience. In the light of this, Wajda's decision to direct Stanislawa Przybyszewska's play *The Danton Affair* at first glance seemed surprising, since its material appeared inconsistent with Wajda's theatrical aims.

Przybyszewska died young in 1935. Her play is primarily an intellectual drama on the philosophy of history, in which human issues are of secondary importance. It deals with the ethics of revolution, which are inspired by reasons and not passion. In the eyes of the author the argument between Danton and Robespierre was not only a tragic conflict between two different human attitudes but above all a historical confrontation of opposed ideals, using the French Revolution as an example. Robespierre represents an adherence to principle, capable at any moment of turning into a dogmatic absolutism that would betray its initial idealism and bring destruction in its wake. Danton on the other hand embodies revolutionary compromise, which in taking man's defective nature into account sullies the moral purity of the 'Idea'. Przybyszewska's sympathies clearly lie with Robespierre, and what he personified was an object of great fascination for her. Nevertheless the conflict of ideas, the main pivot of the drama, remains unresolved to the bitter end. History supplies no answer.

Przybyszewska's talent can be seen in the purely argumentative sequences: the scenes depicting the sittings of the Revolutionary Committee, those in the National Convention and Revolutionary Tribunal. Based on a meticulous study of the documents, the main disputes are political discussions, masterly exegeses of ideological points. This seems a far cry from the artistic temperament that characterizes Wajda's previous films and plays. Yet, on closer scrutiny, this play has qualities that make it a logical extension of his interests. The psychological depth of the main characters and the philosophical content of their encounters are astonishing. None of the figures are schematic and, however long, the disputes are never tedious. The writing and construction reflect the greatness of the times which in turn exudes an influence on the protagonists. The pressure of historical events, manifest in every scene – pressure being one of the main inducements to human action – prevents the play from sliding into arid intellectual debate. Causes become identified with the men who live only for them, ideas are transformed into emotions.

One basic problem facing any director of this play is how to cast it. It requires an unusual number of actors with strong personalities, whose stage presence can confirm the historic charisma of the figures. It so happened that Wajda's old mentor Zygmunt Hübner, now appointed artistic director of the newly opened Teatr Powszechny (Popular Theatre) in Warsaw, had gathered a galaxy of superb actors for his company. What is more, most of them had worked with Wajda before, and Wojciech Pszoniak, who had already made a name for himself in *The Possessed* and in Wajda's film of *The Promised Land*, was available for the part of Robespierre. So rehearsals began with a definite advantage.

The staging of the play presented quite a different problem. From the start, Wajda had established that his production was not going to be a 'historical drama' but 'a drama of history'. But rather than merely updating the text he dispensed almost completely with the conventional stage, which inevitably distances the audience from the action. Instead he decided to transport the action into the auditorium amongst the spectators. The audience were to participate, not merely observe.

Although this was a new approach for Wajda and marked a definite departure from his voluptuous baroque productions, of course it was hardly a new idea as far as world theatre was concerned. Bare stages had already been used in diverse productions and the concept of the action taking place amongst the audience was by no means original. Wajda's decision does not mean however that he deliberately followed in the footsteps of Grotowski,

Andrzej Wajda's 'total theatre'　　　51

18　*The Danton Affair*, Warsaw 1975. Robespierre (Wojciech Pszoniak, second from the left) addresses members of the Committee.

Brook or Barrault. Although well acquainted with the international contemporary theatre scene, Wajda's choice of the bare stage was an independent choice, which evolved from his own interpretation of this particular play.

The number of settings is limited and they are restricted to interiors, with one exception: the prologue outside a baker's shop in a Paris street, where the crowd queuing for bread comments on current events. Their cries and snatches of conversation provide the context for what ensues, revealing that the hungry people are tired of never-ending war and increasing terror, that they anxiously await radical change.

Requiring a totally different kind of setting from the rest of the play, this scene posed certain difficulties in realizing Wajda's concept. One solution considered was for it to take place, authentically, in the street outside the

19 *The Danton Affair*, Warsaw 1975. Danton (Bronislaw Pawlik) before the Revolutionary Tribunal.

theatre, which would also emphasize its dissimilarity from the rest of the play, where there is no counterpart to it in the action. This idea was abandoned for technical reasons. Instead, to distinguish it Wajda used special lighting as well as placing the actors almost out of sight, while the first scene of the play took place simultaneously on a lower level of the set representing Robespierre's apartment.

Designed by Wajda in collaboration with Krystyna Zachwatowicz, the set was constructed in natural wood. The first few rows of seats were removed from the auditorium and in their place a flat wooden platform was laid out, connected by a step to the stage level at the far end. Rows of extra seats were placed on stage so that the audience surrounded the 'acting area' on an upper and lower level. The walls of the auditorium and stage (where the audience were seated) were hung with huge, painted strips of material representing grand architecture; no effort was made to hide their 'operatic' falsification. The only hint of colour was provided by the tricolour flags and rosettes.

From the moment of entering the auditorium it was clear that Wajda's visual style had changed. The obtrusive monumentality of the decor, its almost ascetic simplicity was immediately striking. The enormity, yet simplicity, of the painted wall scenery and the severity of the crude wooden podium was reminiscent of Robespierre's and his followers' disdain for luxury. Prologue apart, lighting effects were used sparingly, in distinct contrast to *The Possessed*. No microphones were used. Not a note of music or amplified sound was to be heard throughout the production. It was an explicit directorial statement: Wajda deliberately eliminated all the technical effects that hitherto had been considered his 'trade mark' to focus on the actors. He released them onto the severe flatness of the stage, dressed in simple costumes, and entrusted them with the play's message: the interplay of ideas, the drama of conscience, the conflict between idealism and morality.

A heavy wooden table was the basic prop used on stage. The members of the Revolutionary Committee met around it to debate, but it also performed many other functions depending on its covering. Upholstered in rich material and scattered with cushions it became the bed of the sybarite Danton. Covered by a coarse white sheet it was the table in Robespierre's apartment. The tricolour flag spread across it rendered it the presidential pulpit at the Convention, and covered with green felt it stood for the judges' rostrum at the Revolutionary Tribunal.

Such minimal details alone were sufficient to conjure up the sharp contrast between the sumptuosity that surrounded Danton and Robespierre's self-inflicted poverty, and to convey the essence of the ideological conflict. But this contrast was personalized by strongly defined behavioural differences in the characterization. Danton, gesticulating broadly, loud-voiced, was easily inflamed and prone to outbursts of vulgarity. Robespierre seemed stiff using gestures sparingly, speaking slowly and precisely, obviously at pains to choose the most accurate and convincing words.

The remaining characters were likewise strongly individualized, the actors giving clearly defined interpretations. But the main dramatic responsibility fell upon the two antagonists, Robespierre and Danton, whose acting styles, however different, nevertheless had one thing in common: a dominance, an undefinable sense of dangerousness that made their impersonation of the great historical figures truly convincing. With the intensity of the acting, which gave a driving force to the action, this impression of credibility made the political rhetoric totally absorbing, both intellectually and emotionally.

20 *The Danton Affair*, Warsaw 1975. Robespierre (Wojciech Pszoniak) confronts Danton (Bronislaw Pawlik).

And the audience involvement was given tangible form by Wajda's decision that the action should take place among the spectators. Seated around the acting area, they began involuntarily to perform certain functions, becoming the jury in the Tribunal or the Deputies in the Convention. Robespierre, Saint-Just, Danton and the other political orators overtly addressed their public speeches to them. Actors seated in the auditorium balconies, which became the Public Gallery of the courtroom and the Convention, shouted out in reply, giving the illusion that the voices of the people were coming from the audience.

The moral issue raised by *The Danton Affair* lay neither solely with the conscience of the Revolutionary leaders, nor with the deliberations of the

Convention, Tribunal or Committee of Public Safety, but in the hearts of everyone present. However, the theatrical performance offered no solution to two dilemmas that had been left unsolved by history. The play might be weighted in Robespierre's favour, yet in the final scene, after the execution of Danton, the surviving titan of the Revolution remains alone with his conscience and at the mercy of his own doubts, gripped by a metaphysical fear of the growing and uncontrollable Terror. Soon it will engulf him also, as Danton foretold on his way to the guillotine, and in this conclusion Robespierre, the apparent victor and triumphant leader, staggering beneath the ruins of his own ideals, stands revealed as the next victim. Even so, in the silence that follows Danton's fading cries, this unimpeachable man places his hands firmly on the shoulders of Saint-Just. Refusing to give in to human weakness he seals the victory for the Revolution together with his own fate. The final image confirms that the call of duty – to the Revolution and to history – is higher than individual morality or personal survival. Full of idealistic blunders, even fatal mistakes, this Revolution still changed the face of the earth forever.

Although the style of this production was very different from *The Possessed* and *November Night*, it completed Andrzej Wajda's 'total theatre' cycle. In *The Danton Affair* Wajda had discovered how to achieve the same intensity of expression with the bare minimum of technical effects and decor. Where earlier he was drawn to a baroque form now he seemed to be looking for a classical purity of line. One could still detect his painter's eye, but it had been subjected to greater rigour in order to give a modern and original interpretation to an important work dealing with universal values.

The continuing relevance of Wajda's 1975 production of *The Danton Affair* can be indicated by its reception when restaged – directed by the author of this book – in three contexts that varied both historically and culturally: in 1977 in Sofia, Bulgaria; in the autumn of 1981 at the Teatr Wybrzeze, where Wajda had made his theatrical debut; and in 1982 in Trieste, Italy. The relationship of these versions to the original may be likened to replicas in painting. The overall outline of the Warsaw production was retained, together with the design. However, the effects upon each of the three audiences differed so widely that the significance of the production changed radically. The Bulgarians, used to the ideological orthodoxy of Marxism, were deeply moved by the concept of Revolution as a tragic dialectic. What impressed the Italian audience most was the way the play illustrated the machinations that led to the Terror. However, the most interesting response was conditioned by the circumstances surrounding the 1981 Gdansk production. The play opened immediately after the strikes that started the Solidarity trade union movement. The pervading atmosphere of agitation could

21 Danton (Gérard Depardieu) before the Revolutionary Tribunal in the film version, *Danton* (1982).

literally be called revolutionary. The play became at once a running commentary on actual events, and a warning that certain elements, if unleashed, could get out of control. Although siding with the Revolution, it did not provoke simple affirmation from the audience. Instead, bitterly and controversially, it exposed the age-old conflict between man's desire for perfect freedom and the imperfectability of human nature.

Andrzej Wajda himself returned to *The Danton Affair* with his 1982 French film, *Danton*, which was also based on Przybyszewska's play. The actors were Polish and French, but Robespierre was played once more by Wojciech Pszoniak. Influenced by topical events (the imposition of martial law in

Poland), Wajda gave the play an emphasis radically different from its accepted philosophical viewpoint. By eliminating the more human traits in Robespierre he turned him into a demagogue, the fanatic idealist of the Revolution. On the other hand he emphasized Danton's sympathetic features by representing him as champion of those who seek a more human face in revolution. This shift of focus was reinforced by the change in medium. On screen, it was obviously easier to show the Revolutionary masses, and the film was more violent than the play. It seemed more in line with the stage version of *The Possessed* than with its own theatrical counterpart. The play featured intellectual reasoning, the film depended mainly on emotional effect.

This interpretation created much controversy, especially in France where the Left resented this distorted picture of the 'Great Revolution'. The French President François Mitterrand left the theatre before the end of the film at a private viewing. The left-wing French press found Wajda's interpretation of the French Revolution verging on caricature and were especially offended by the characterization of Robespierre. The right-wing critics on the other hand praised the film's demonstration of the fact that demagogy and totalitarianism can lurk behind the façade of revolutionary ideals. By contrast the Polish public saw the film as a distinct metaphor of their current situation, where ideological and political so-called 'reasons of state' are at variance with human needs, happiness and personal freedom.[5]

4 The dilemmas of liberty: *Abandoned by Reason* and *The Emigrants*

Antonio Buero Vallejo's play *Abandoned by Reason* featured the painter Goya. An anti-fascist writing in General Franco's Spain, Vallejo's political sub-text was readily appreciated when the play first appeared in the Polish translation in 1974; and Tadeusz Lomnicki, an obvious choice for the leading part, had been encouraging Wajda to direct it. However, it was only after *The Danton Affair*, when Lomnicki was made director of his own theatre, Teatr Na Woli (Wola District Theatre) in Warsaw, that the project came to fruition.

Set in the 'Quinta del Sordo' ('Deaf Man's Villa'), its walls covered with Goya's 'black' paintings – sometimes interpreted as the expression of insanity – the action spans the final days before Goya's exile in December 1823. Everyone is at risk. In the eyes of the fanatical Royal Volunteers (monarchist vigilantes) anyone could be a covert liberal sympathizer. Despite the warnings of his friends, the deaf and half-mad old man remains passive, oblivious to the rampant terror in his country, until the volunteers attack and plunder the house. Humiliated, frightened, he finally decides to emigrate.

It is no coincidence that the main character is a great painter. Notwithstanding its political theme, which establishes parallels between the historical situation and contemporary repression, the play is primarily a treatise on art. Artistic creativity is portrayed as the embodiment of human liberty, the flight of the individual from physical and spiritual captivity, the artist's task being to guard this liberty. His duty to his country, and to humanity at large, is to propagate freedom through his art: a position that has much in common with Wajda's own outlook on art and which forms one of the main components of his artistic philosophy. The title is taken from one of Goya's sketches called *Los Caprichos: Abandoned by Reason – Fancy Produces Monsters*; and the play applies their vision to the social situation in Spain. The abandonment of reason liberates the demons of violence, intolerance, and brutal stupidity symbolized by the Inquisition and Absolute Monarchy. Another of Goya's paintings is entitled *Divine Reason Spares No One* – and these are the words that Goya himself utters at the moment of greatest violence. Thus in the light of Vallejo's drama, those strange, dark paintings from the 'Deaf Man's Villa' are not the ravings of illness, deafness and senility, but reason's impassioned protest against the evil teeming around it.

A striking feature of the play is the way it uses the concept of deafness to draw the audience into the nightmare existence of the sick protagonist. When the other characters converse with Goya, we observe their gestures, see their lips move. But we do not hear their voices. Only when Goya leaves the stage do the speeches become audible as, metaphorically, we regain our hearing. Whenever the painter reappears we hear the flapping of invisible monsters' wings and weird noises. Words, sounding like a kind of running commentary, spoken by someone unknown, reach us from afar.

Working again with Krystyna Zachwatowicz, Wajda designed a set that facilitated a kind of close contact between actors and spectators as in *The Danton Affair*. The main action took place on a narrow bridge that protruded into the auditorium, upon which, in a dim shaft of light, one could discern a table and some armchairs. The rear of the stage represented the actual interior of the villa with Goya's paintings of the 'Black Period' projected onto the walls; others stood on easels. The composition was intended to symbolize the permanence of art, its superiority to the folly of life on earth.

A vital element of the play is the pervasive atmosphere of unremitting menace and omnipresent fear. Wajda emphasized this atmosphere by introducing a group of volunteers permanently into the action. An on-stage audience, they spy on the proceedings, watching from the shadows, lying in wait for a sign, a word that would betray Goya — or any of the actual spectators — as a suspected liberal. When the word is given the most lurid scene ensues. Goya is forcibly dressed in the clown's costume of the heretic, mirroring his own drawings of the *auto-da-fé*. Tied to a chair, he is made to watch while the soldiers rape Leocadia, his companion in old age, his housekeeper and mistress.

Because of Wajda's personal interest in painting this scene in particular was visually vivid — a composite of Goya's etchings, which had been used as a basis for the blocking throughout the play. At one point, for instance, the stage composition was an almost identical replica of the sketch from which the play takes its title. The man asleep at the table was Goya himself, the monsters surrounding him were the volunteers. Elsewhere Leocadia, while sweeping the floor, would suddenly become a witch on a broomstick, or the artist's dead daughter would appear as one of the young girls out of his sketches, representing all the purity that was doomed to corruption in an evil world. Of all the ghouls of Goya's hallucinations that filled the stage, this daughter, with whose death he could never come to terms, dominated the action. He conjured her up again and again, sometimes as a child of innocence, at other times as a wrinkled old hag, representing death.

This was the most pictorial of Wajda's productions. The subtle lighting played a large part. It created a feeling of space, filled with varying shades of gloom, from which emerged human faces, eyes, and fragments of Goya's

22 *Abandoned by Reason,* Warsaw 1976. Goya (Tadeusz Lomnicki) dressed for the *auto-da-fé* by the Royal Volunteers.

The dilemmas of liberty

23 *Abandoned by Reason*, Warsaw 1976. Doña Leocadia (Lidia Korsakowna) as the witch in Goya's vision (Goya: Tadeusz Lomnicki).

paintings. Stylistically it bridged the gap between productions such as *November Night*, with its wealth of theatrical effects, and the ascetic *Danton Affair* – taking a step back, as it were, in order to draw conclusions from past experience and explore some of the theatrical possibilities passed over in his creative evolution. As a work of transition, *Abandoned by Reason* should be seen as indicative of those moments of reflection and introspection out of which an artist formulates a new departure – and the next play Wajda took on was very different from any of his previous stage work.

After the allegorical, visual, Spanish drama, he chose *The Emigrants*, a modern tragicomedy by Slawomir Mrozek, the greatest living Polish playwright. Mrozek, who has lived in Paris for many years, not only sums up his own experience in the play but offers a deep analysis of the psychological and moral phenomenon of emigration, in the form of a witty comedy. Polish and East European audiences could also catch certain political allusions, but these are not the dramatist's priority. Quite the opposite, to stress the universality of his theme Mrozek does not even give his two main characters names. Nor does he inform us where the action is taking place. He presents a model situation: two men share lodgings, or rather a tiny room under the stairs, somewhere in Europe. One has left his homeland for political motives, the other for financial reasons. Where they have come from, or where they actually live now, is unimportant. AA and XX, men with no name or nationality, represent the essence of the *émigré*'s predicament, any *émigré*. The construction of the play is simple, without shifts in time or place. Yet its universality is highly ambiguous as the wide variety of interpretations offered by productions in different countries indicates. Mrozek combines burlesque with tragedy, drama with farce. The play contains comic elements, as well as those depicting the bleaker side of human existence – a combination also characteristic of Samuel Beckett's writing. Indeed *The Emigrants* is clearly related to Beckett's plays, and specifically to *Endgame*. What is important to Beckett, however, is the existential, psychological and emotional drama of the main characters, whom he casts into an abstract world. Mrozek is interested in the social aspects of the situation and places his characters in a real, though no less absurd world. The basis of Wajda's interpretation was extremely simple though it raised highly equivocal questions. It is New Year's Eve, people all over the world are thinking with hope of the future, making resolutions and plans to improve their lives or realize their dreams. But for AA and XX there are no hopes or dreams. The New Year comes with one man snoring and the other weeping: two different facets of each man's helplessness *vis-à-vis* his fate. To Wajda, however, *The Emigrants* was primarily a debate on the concept of freedom and the diverse ways it is understood and interpreted. The play deals very concisely with an extremely pertinent question: What is freedom? Is real freedom abstract, spiritual, and intellectual as experienced by AA? Or is it existentialist and carefree as experienced by XX? The author, considering there is much to be said in favour of both, leaves us to make up our own minds on the subject.

As it stands, the play is so crystal-clear in its construction that there seems to be no need for a director, especially one so imaginative and creative as Wajda, the painter, the 'effects' specialist, who had made a name for dramas of human passion depicted on an epic scale. Construct a set, employ two good actors, and the rest would happen on its own. However, Wajda's staging in the studio (Scena Kameralna) of the Stary Teatr in Cracow expanded the meaning of the play in a way that brought out a variety of unexpected nuances. For a start his production began in a very original way: outside the

The dilemmas of liberty 63

24   *The Emigrants*, Cracow 1976. View of the set. XX: Jerzy Binczycki; AA: Jerzy Stuhr.

theatre, in the street. Brightly coloured lights twinkled over the gate and along the passage leading to the entrance of the theatre, beckoning the spectators to enter. On the floor lay a red carpet and eye-catching advertisements in illuminated showcases hung on the walls. Outside the door, which was illuminated with a bright neon sign, stood two life-size cardboard figures, one of each actor. Their arms were brimming with packages, cartons of luxury goods were piled at their feet. Wajda's intention was that the spectator should follow XX's homeward route to the tiny room he shares with

AA, through the festively lit town. But though some Polish critics actually deliberated whether the illuminations were a successful reproduction of the 'bright lights' in Western town-centres, this was quite beside the point. The shoddiness of the decorations, evident on closer inspection, was wholly in line with the concept behind the overall setting. The spectators were seeing them through the eyes of the primitive XX. Like him, fascinated and attracted as well as alienated by the attributes of this colourful world, they were meant to find them bewildering, unfamiliar and even threatening.

On finally reaching the theatre, somewhat dazed by the pop music blaring from all sides, one was confronted by a huge painting. It depicted a group of immigrants being welcomed with open arms by the Statue of Liberty . . . The auditorium was equally transformed. On entering, the first impression was that of a cinema. Commercials were being shown on a huge black-framed screen that had been erected on stage, and the play began with 'the credits' as in a film. Then the screen was lifted but the black frame remained, retaining the cinematic illusion. Stretched across it was a gauze. With the help of lighting this gave a misty effect and the impression of watching a film, slightly out of focus, as the action began.

The screen was not merely the idea of a film director, it had a dual, specifically theatrical purpose. On the one hand, it served to create distance, to intensify the impression that events taking place on stage were one step removed from reality. On the other hand, it brought the audience in closer, to watch the action more intensely. We have become so used to the 'close-up' in cinema, that we expect to see magnified and detailed events taking place before our very eyes. The screen, in this case, did not fulfil such a function. Yet the power of suggestion created the illusion that we were watching a film rather than a play, with the result that the audience paid more attention to detail than is usual in the theatre.

From the actors' viewpoint the screen fulfilled yet another function. The lighting, confined to the inside of the black frame on the actors' side, enabled the audience to see them but not vice versa. The actors, therefore, were totally isolated. It gave them a feeling of being really alone within the four walls of the little room, and undoubtedly helped them create the electric atmosphere of solitude so pertinent to the play.

The actual set was an extremely realistic representation of a typical cellar in a big apartment block with its tangle of pipes and scattered junk. The lighting – the effect of a naked light bulb in the first act; the dim flickering flame of candles and lighted matches in the second act – accentuated this realism. Even the sound effects were real: a recording of noises in the pipes; laughter, singing, and stamping from the floor above. The play began with the sound of approaching footsteps and XX appeared, clambering down from some-

The dilemmas of liberty

25 *The Emigrants*, Cracow 1976. View of the set. XX: Jerzy Binczycki; AA: Jerzy Stuhr.

where above. He entered the little room, took off his rustling nylon raincoat, and with a characteristic gesture ran a comb through his hair. Hovering undecidedly for a moment, he finally spoke the first line of the play: ''Ere I am.' As played by Jerzy Binczycki this brief opening sequence conveyed the unmistakable image of a simple workman living in a strange and foreign land with nothing but primitive, unrealistic dreams. He was touchingly straightforward. At the same time his naive simplicity was combined with traits of inborn bigotry. Obviously deeply homesick, there was a tragic sadness about him. By contrast Jerzy Stuhr, in the role of his 'partner' AA, presented a neurotic intellectual clinging to outside appearances, attempting to salvage his crumbling ideals even at a price of self-deception.

26 *The Emigrants*, Cracow 1976. AA (Jerzy Stuhr) discovers XX's (XX: Jerzy Binczycki) savings hidden in the toy dog.

Wajda's realistic treatment, as apparent in the acting as in the design of the set, was stylistically closer to his production of *A Hatful of Rain* than to Mrozek's absurdist vision. Although the play veers towards universal allegory and the grotesque in the style of Beckett, Wajda scrutinized it for real-life truth, both social and psychological. While retaining all the comedy he emphasized the tragic and, above all, the human element. He brought out its metaphoric nature by using detail, rather than abstract generalization. For instance in the last scene AA, driven to despair, tears up all the money he has saved over the years. In the play this can only be a symbolic gesture for it would be difficult to destroy a thick wad of bank notes by tearing them into tiny pieces in the brief moment of madness allowed by the text. However in Wajda's version the desperate man, rather than tearing up the money, flushes it down the lavatory — a real gesture of irrevocable destruction. Characteristically the lavatory, hidden by flimsy partition, had already 'played its part' earlier on in the play. XX used it (accompanied by realistic sound effects) while AA delivered his gushing speech on the great literary work he intended to write about the 'ideal slave'. This brutal realism had the power of a sharp, metaphorical summary, evident also at the end of the play when XX attempts to hang himself. Instead of standing on a chair, as indicated by the author, he stands on the unstable edge of an upturned table. The scene originally was more grotesquely absurd than psychologically probable, but now it took on an element of danger and actual threat of death. The tragicomedy became a tragedy whilst the symbolic figures became real people.

Wajda's characteristic use of 'counterpoint' was much in evidence in this production, particularly in the final scene. After his abortive suicide attempt XX throws himself onto his bed. Shielding his eyes from the light, AA clambers onto the table. For an instant we are led to believe that he too is about to attempt suicide, but he merely retrieves his belt. He gets down and switches off the light. Only then do we hear his hysterical sobbing, accompanied by XX's snoring, and in that darkness the cellar door mysteriously opens. Beyond it a strange light is glowing and the gentle strains of a Polonaise can be heard from afar. The music — *A Farewell to the Homeland* by Michal Kleofas Oginski — with its sentimental significance for every Pole, relates the elusive ideal of freedom and the hope for the future denied by the figures on stage directly to the experience of the audience.[1] The main link between this and Wajda's other productions is not the coloured lights, nor the screen, nor any of the other characteristic, imaginative ideas of the director, but the use of this soft piece of music to emphasize issues of nationalism and humanity.

Although on the face of it *Abandoned by Reason* and *The Emigrants* are very different plays, both in content and form as well as scenic realization, they deal with a common subject: freedom. One is concerned with the inner freedom of an artist faced with political oppression; the other with the existential freedom of the individual torn from his social and cultural environment. These two extremes demarcate the theme that unites all

Wajda's work. The definition of liberty and the exploration of its implications is the basic preoccupation of both his theatrical productions and his films, and provides the essential link in his development from *Ashes and Diamonds* to his interpretations of *The Possessed*, *November Night* and *The Danton Affair*. What distinguishes Wajda's analysis is that the various dilemmas of freedom are always portrayed in a political and historical context; and this makes his theatrical voice a significant contribution to the great twentieth-century dispute on the subject of human freedom and its boundaries.

5 Madness, love and death: *Nastasya Filippovna* and *Crime and Punishment*

It was Dostoyevsky's novels that provided Wajda with the material for his three most significant theatrical productions: *The Possessed* (1971), *Nastasya Filippovna* (based on *The Idiot*, 1977) and finally *Crime and Punishment* (1984). These clearly indicate how Wajda's ideas on 'total theatre' evolved from epic breadth to a more intimate style.

The success of *The Possessed* led Wajda to consider adapting *The Idiot* for television. Nothing came of this, and in 1975 after *The Danton Affair* he began rehearsals for a stage version at the Teatr Maly in Warsaw. The original television adaptation, which provided the script, followed the outline of the novel fairly closely. But as rehearsals progressed it went through successive changes. Wajda applied the same principle, recommended by Dostoyevsky, that he had used in *The Possessed* – extracting a key episode and expanding it to incorporate the main themes of the novel. Already, during this early phase, the final concept had taken shape. The action became restricted to two characters – Rogozhin and Prince Myshkin – but with the focus on a figure who never appeared: the fascinating Nastasya. Wajda became progressively drawn to this idea, but at this point did not know how to realize the complexity of Dostoyevsky's material in such a radically simplified form.

Almost two years passed between the preliminary rehearsals in Warsaw and the production in Cracow, and the intervening work on *Abandoned by Reason* and *The Emigrants* offered some potential solutions. The projection of an abnormal interior state, in which the phantasmagoria of a sensitive mind revealed the moral essence of a sick society, together with the claustrophobic relationship of Mrozek's duo in their enclosed space, clearly related to the problems of staging a 'two-hander' based on *The Idiot*. He decided on a strange venue: instead of a proper stage, a shabby room used for storing old sets. The atmosphere in this gloomy, long room with dusty window-panes had a decisive influence on the early rehearsals. Without much adaptation, it could represent Rogozhin's apartment, and this immediately brought to mind two central episodes described in the novel: Myshkin's visit after Nastasya's murder and the exchange of crucifixes between Myshkin and Rogozhin. As a result it was on these 'scenes' and with just two actors, Jerzy Radziwilowicz as Myshkin and Jan Nowicki as Rogozhin, that work began.

Wajda also decided that the rehearsals should be open to the public. There was no ideological rationale for this, and it was never intended to co-opt the spectators for the action or to use them as catalysts. Instead, as he explained when the series of twenty-seven open rehearsals commenced on 8 January 1977,

> In my opinion, contemporary theatre in its search for new forms and new relationships between actors and audience, should consider the function of rehearsals and their capacity of becoming performances in their own right. Could not rehearsals, which are an enriching and unforgettable experience for us, and which we coyly hide from the public, be of interest to that public? Personally I always enjoy watching craftsmen ply their trade. Why then, should they not be interested in my work?[1]

This, of course, was slightly disingenuous. The novelty of the experiment for all concerned clearly affected the nature of the process, though ultimately in unexpected ways. The presence of spectators not only provided a sounding-board for the actors or a testing-ground for directorial ideas, but was supposed to inject the same psychological uncertainty as the fear of failure that had proved so valuable in creating the atmospheric tension of *The Possessed*. The production was to emerge slowly before the very eyes of a paying audience of 120 people, with the only known quantity being Dostoyevsky's novel *The Idiot*. The actors had to reveal what they usually hid from the audience. Their doubts and inadequacies were publicly displayed, becoming an ingredient of the performance. The director in turn had to put forward concepts that had not yet totally crystallized, often having to 'back out' and search for new ideas before the critical gaze of an audience. The spectators, mainly students and theatre fans, also had a vastly different experience from that of the customary visit to the theatre. Used to being presented with the finished product, they now witnessed the uncertainty, the searching, the actors' struggle for control of their limbs and voices and the director's attempt to 'forge' a production out of the vast material of his thoughts and ideas.

Once the initial inhibitions of the cast were overcome, however, it was found that the presence of an audience began to have an undesired effect. Instead of posing a threat and thereby inspiring the actors to do better, spectators seemed blindly to accept all that was put before them. Such was their fascination with the craft of theatre itself that they ceased to consider the end result which was the object of the exercise. They endorsed all new ideas (conceived at private meetings before rehearsals) with such uncritical approval that the sensation of progress towards the final goal was lost. This demoralized the actors, since as Jan Nowicki put it, 'For the actor, the opening night is the first confrontation with the enemy, the audience, which must be mastered. If the auditorium is packed with friends from the very start, there is no one to battle against, no one to convince or influence. It is quite disarming.'[2]

Madness, love and death

In response Wajda decided to suspend open rehearsals, but in reverting to normal working methods he also returned to a more conventional approach to the problem of adaptation. One thing that had become apparent during the course of the public rehearsals was that the layered richness of the novel could not be condensed into a single theme. The original conception was shelved and Wajda began to explore the material on a completely different basis. With the participation of seventeen actors, he devised an ensemble scene, where Myshkin sees his entire life pass before him in a vision which precedes an epileptic fit. This scene was also a theatrical exemplification of the metaphorical layer of the novel: Myshkin-Christ 'performs the Stations of the Cross'. At each juncture a suitably adapted scene from the novel was inserted.

However, this experiment too was clearly an unsatisfactory compromise. The structural difficulty of condensing the whole novel into a normal performance time produced a visual paraphrase which was thematically inadequate, while the sheer volume of material distracted from the psychology of the protagonist which the visionary scenes were intended to exemplify.

Once more Wajda returned to his starting point and the final conception for the production took shape during one of the long, nocturnal rehearsals. Stating 'I am sure of three things: this room is perfect, the casting is right and the text is good', Wajda abandoned all responsibility for the script to the actors. After outlining the general idea behind the production, he left the two original actors to create their respective characters from the entire contents of the novel. A new improvisation entitled *Nastasya Filippovna* came into being. Although this was based on Dostoyevsky's novel *The Idiot*, the actors were left entirely free to choose their own text and create their own scenes, reactions and emotions – a terrifying degree of freedom, that carried over through the whole run of the piece.

The improvisation begins with the following scene: Myshkin comes to Rogozhin's darkened apartment where the latter sits with the corpse of his beloved Nastasya Filippovna whom he has murdered. From behind the velvet curtain where her body lies hidden only the white shape of a bed can be detected, on which something glimmers – the wedding gown Nastasya had donned for her marriage to Prince Myshkin. As the night vigil begins, the phantoms of the past haunt their minds and madness hovers over both men who had each, in his own way, destroyed his love. The game of passion, hate and death begins. They are both totally alone, in the deepest sense of the word.

The large rectangular room had two doors in one of the longer walls and on the opposite side three large windows. Diffused lights placed behind them

27 *Nastasya Filippovna*, Cracow 1977. Prince Myshkin (Jerzy Radziwilowicz) and Rogozhin (Jan Nowicki, on the floor).

gave a natural impression of St Petersburg's 'white nights'. Between the windows hung an icon with a red lamp and the portrait of an elderly man who could be taken for Rogozhin's father. A sofa stood beneath the portrait, a small table and armchair beneath the icon and between the doors a wardrobe. In front of the sofa stood a heavy desk and armchair, in the centre of the room a round table and two chairs. Marks on the walls show where a large number of pictures once hung and have recently been taken down. Only one remains – Holbein's unusual depiction of Christ above the door, as described by Dostoyevsky, illuminated by a flickering, dim light. The audience were seated along the wall with the doors and on elevated platforms at the two far ends of the room. At one end they sat on either side of a green velvet curtain behind which is the bedroom, where the body of the murdered Nastasya lies. Surrounding the acting area on three sides, the spectators were literally enclosed in the characters' room – a logical development of the 'total theatre' design of *The Danton Affair*, which provided intimate contact with the actors in a physical context that was realistic, rather than the artificial extension of the setting into a conventional auditorium.

The action – if one can use such a term in this case – had begun even before the audience entered. When the doors were opened to admit the public, the two protagonists were already 'on stage' and the 'play' in progress. In accordance with the novel Myshkin should be seen to arrive at the apartment, and this was originally rehearsed. Rogozhin peered through the window, searching for Myshkin outside the building, and brought him in from the street. Once it was decided to improvise, this idea was abandoned because its purely scenic realism distracted from the psychological focus. During rehearsals the actors discovered that it took them some time to achieve the desired emotional climate. However, if the whole 'performance' could be repeated, the right levels of intensity were reached the second or even the third time around. This was clearly impracticable with an audience present, but in place of conventional warm-up exercises Wajda had them in character and playing out their improvisation each night for some time before the spectators entered. The only blocking requirement was that at this point they should hold a specific position while the audience seated themselves and their eyes got accustomed to the dimness. Rogozhin, his shirt open, his feet bare, lies on the sofa. Prince Myshkin, in a spotless white linen suit, is sitting in the armchair by the desk in an exceedingly uncomfortable position. He is extremely tense, suggesting the shape of a huge, white question mark. He stays motionless in the dim light, listening as Rogozhin gabbles incoherently, his words barely audible. Rogozhin begins to describe some event, breaking off to mention a name here and there, an odd word, a sum of money, or repeating fragments of a conversation. As Rogozhin, Nowicki was free to choose his lines from any part of the novel. The text offers vast possibilities. At each performance he could pick out what he felt he needed to say. But even though his fevered imagination escapes logic and confuses chronology, the subject is always obsessively the same – Nastasya Filippovna. In trying to relive all the events connected with her, remembering her gestures, recalling words, it was as if Rogozhin were making a 'confession' to the corpse of his beloved whom he stabbed to death.

This continues until all the audience have settled into silence and the doors have been closed. As Rogozhin's muttered tirade continues Prince Myshkin's fists press into the armrests of his chair, almost forcing him to his feet with the effort to interrupt, yet he seems incapacitated from speaking for fear of what a question might reveal. Finally he manages to blurt out the words that served as a key to the whole production: 'Is Nastasya Filippovna with you?'

The scene that ensues was inspired by the final part of the novel and has been dubbed by critics 'one of the darkest scenes in world literature'. It is the fullest exemplification of the moral and philosophic content of *The Idiot* and the culmination of its action. The two rivals/friends meet in this gloomy room in Rogozhin's bourgeois apartment. For the past months the violent Rogozhin and the saintly Prince Myshkin have been competing for the love of Nastasya Filippovna. Nastasya was about to marry the Prince but at the last minute ran off with Rogozhin. Now Myshkin has come to look for her. He is however ignorant of the fact that Rogozhin has killed her, in a crazed fit of jealousy: her body lies in the same room behind the drawn curtain. The final climax has been reached: the extraordinary, enigmatic woman is dead, Rogozhin will have to accept a terrible punishment for his crime of passion, and Prince Myshkin will end his pilgrimage, reminiscent of Christ's way to the cross.

This scene contains the basic material for the play. It is still improvised, nothing has been set or blocked, but in this fragment the text remained the same at each performance. It is the only scene where Dostoyevsky's dialogue (with only a few small cuts) is spoken in full and in its original sequence.

Up to this point Rogozhin had kept his voice down, insisting that the Prince do likewise for fear of detection. But at the end of this scene, unhinged by the memory of an incident when Nastasya slapped the face of an officer — an absolute stranger — Rogozhin begins to scream incomprehensibly. This sudden loss of self-control and the totally uncalled-for nature of the outburst initiate the 'insane sequence' that formed the longest and most significant episode in the play.

Rogozhin's raving, accompanied by a wild succession of memories, a feverish recall of events both important and commonplace, begins visibly to affect the Prince whose debilitating illness has given him a certain predisposition to melancholia. Although in the novel the Prince is described as merely passive, occupied in trying to calm Rogozhin down, this interpretation is justified from Dostoyevsky's reference to Myshkin being found in a trance the next morning when the door is broken down. So, in the production, he too succumbs to madness as the vigil over the corpse becomes a nightmare of conversations with the dead woman, phantoms and hallucinations.

Rogozhin's madness is monothematic, only concerning Nastasya. By contrast Myshkin's insanity takes a philosophic form. His wish to do good on his arrival in Russia has resulted in murder; his belief in total truthfulness has

Madness, love and death

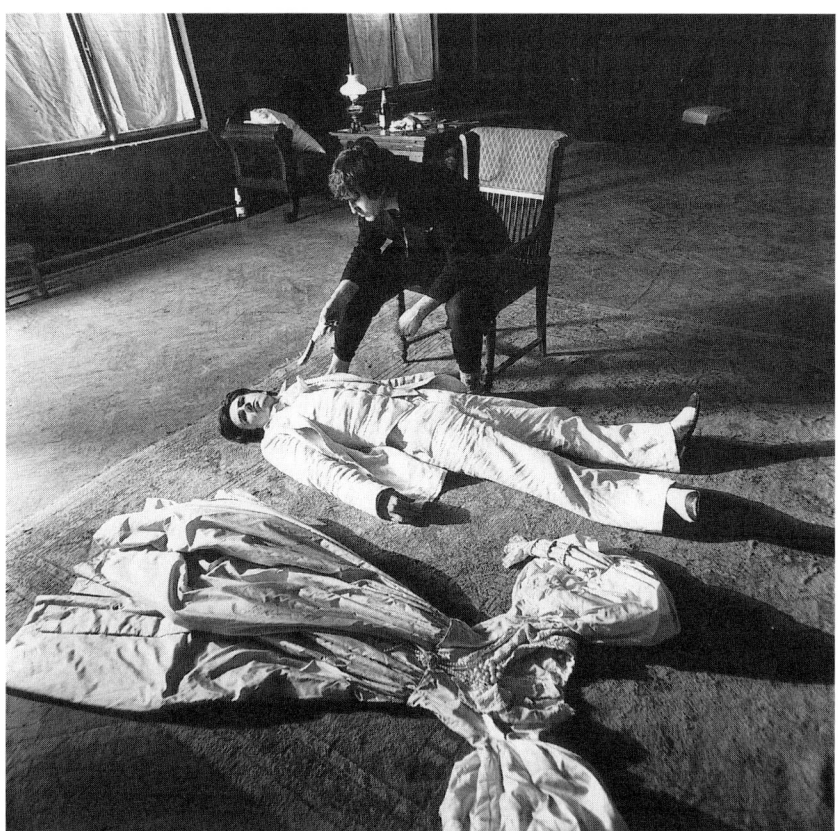

28 *Nastasya Filippovna*, Cracow 1977. Rogozhin (Jan Nowicki) over the prostrate Prince Myshkin (Jerzy Radziwilowicz).

made a fiasco of human values, causing destruction and undermining universal principles. Pondering over the irrationality of existence and the ironic absurdity of his actions, in the role of Myshkin Radziwilowicz was free to voice all the moral and religious issues that appear in the pages of *The Idiot*.

Since no performance duplicated another, the requirements of the dialogue altered every night. Each actor, depending on the flow of events during a given performance, might draw on any information about the character he portrays – or indeed the other characters – speaking completely different lines from any used before and varying situations that had previously been established. The only guiding rule was that the inspiration be grounded in Dostoyevsky's text. His partner would then take up the new theme or embark upon one of his own, to which in turn the other would respond.

This was the principle of improvisation taken to an extreme. None of the situations were 'blocked'. On the contrary, the object was to avoid repeating any previously adopted dramatic resolutions, even when the ideas conceived during rehearsals seemed not only interesting, but also irreplaceable. When the prejudice towards retaining 'successful' actions was overcome, the next solutions found often proved more creative. At the same time the most interesting effect and the greatest tension, achieved at one of the all-night rehearsals, was never quite reached again during the public performances. However, the plan was not to repeat a single situation, and to ensure this Wajda observed all rehearsals with a little bell to hand, which he rang every time the actors engaged in a sequence that had been enacted at any point before.

Although each performance of *Nastasya Filippovna* was different, the action can be divided into three essential parts.

1. Prince Myshkin visits Rogozhin (this is the last scene in the novel)
2. Psychodrama (improvisation).
3. The outcome: Rogozhin is prepared for his exile to Siberia and Myshkin becomes mad.

The action in the first section is relatively easy to describe. It comprises:

a) Rogozhin's monologue. He is seated on the sofa as he speaks. Myshkin sits speechless and motionless in the armchair.
b) The discovery of Nastasya's body behind the curtain. After Rogozhin's outburst ('and that cadet . . . that cadet leapt up . . .') and a long pause, Myshkin finally asks: 'Is Nastasya Filoppovna with you?' Rogozhin then leads him to the body. Myshkin's strength fails him and he cannot move.
c) The two men prepare for the long night vigil ahead: Rogozhin carries the Prince to the sofa. He seeks Myshkin's advice on how to conceal the presence of the body in the apartment. He then locks the front door.
d) The start of madness: Prince Myshkin, pacing back and forth, presses Rogozhin for details of the murder and urges him to describe his last night with Nastasya.

The pace of the last sequence becomes increasingly agitated and chaotic, setting the stage for the improvisation that is to follow. As a rule fragments of dialogue, taken from the very first scene in the novel where Myshkin and Rogozhin meet for the first time, were used as a transition from the first part to the second.

e) They recall their first meeting in the train: their conversation begins with Rogozhin's question: 'It's cold, isn't it?' This would either lead to further dialogue between them, or to the Prince's fragmented reminiscences of his stay in Switzerland from where he has just returned. Now the actual improvisation begins. Although nothing was set definitely, it is possible to describe some of the alternatives.
f) Myshkin approaches the door (forgetting that it is locked). He notices the Holbein painting hanging above the door, stops, and begins a monologue in which he relates his feelings on the subject of religion that gives us an insight into religious feeling in Russia. As he listens, Rogozhin takes a knife and creeps up on Myshkin. His attempt to strike him results in the Prince having an epileptic fit.

Madness, love and death

g) Another version of this sequence could be a conversation, evolving from remarks on Rogozhin's father's portrait, about Rogozhin's family. (For Myshkin they represented a specific type of Russian.)

h) The exchanging of crosses: Rogozhin stops Myshkin from leaving ('Stay with me a while, Leo Nikolayovitch . . .'). He proceeds to tell the Prince of his ambivalent feelings towards him and suggests they exchange crosses, as a sign of brotherhood.

i) The exchange of crosses leads to the 'game with the armchair': Rogozhin leads Myshkin to the empty armchair in the corner of the room and behaves as if he were introducing Myshkin to his mother who is seated there. Myshkin responds and kneels in front of the empty armchair. As a rule this scene would be brutally interrupted by Rogozhin breaking the illusion and laughing at the Prince's stupidity.

j) The scene with 'Rogozhin's mother' might lead to a flow of memories, recollections of Nastasya Filippovna, whom Rogozhin had also introduced to his mother. This sequence could contain any of the dialogue from the many scenes in the novel appertaining to Nastasya. Myshkin would sometimes take on the role of the dead woman, as they re-enacted the scenes in which she figured. In these sequences her wedding dress (brought out from behind the curtain) and other 'props' would be used — for example a copy of Soloviov's *History of Russia*, which Nastasya had ordered Rogozhin to read in order to further his limited education. Rogozhin would sit in the corner and, ignoring Myshkin, read aloud from this book.

k) This might present the opportunity for Myshkin to begin his own separate action simultaneously. For example he could inspect the apartment and its contents, speaking to himself all the while. The subject of this monologue would differ, although he often aired his views on capital punishment. (Myshkin speaks of this at length at the start of the novel.)

At each performance the order of these sequences could differ and new themes and solutions might be introduced. However it was characteristic that towards the end of the performance the two protagonists become increasingly separate. The dialogue turns rather to monologue; the Prince becomes more and more introverted and it seems that Rogozhin's words no longer reach him.

The final sequence follows:

l) Rogozhin prepares himself for his punishment: no longer listening to the Prince's monologue, he cleans his boots, sews money into the lining of his coat and sometimes eats or drinks. During this business the Prince slides to the floor where he sits and gabbles incoherently.

m) The ending: Rogozhin flings the door open wide, letting in a bright ray of sunlight. He approaches Myshkin and beckons him to leave the apartment. They exit together.

From the above description, which outlines elements of the story and dialogue, it is not evident that one of the production's outstanding characteristics was its physical intensity. There was much varied stage activity, performed mainly by Rogozhin. For instance, he would pace the room, leap onto the window sill in order to talk to someone in the street below, creep up on or dance around Myshkin, wrestle with him, eat and drink seated at the table, even simulate urinating onto the floor.

To sum up it must be emphasized that, since this production was an improvisation and the course of the action lay entirely in the actors' hands, it is extremely difficult to give a precise account of what occurred on stage. The best that can be achieved is to build up a composite picture.

A performance lasted one and a half hours. A clock on the wall told the actual time, and the chimes every quarter gave the actors a chance to keep a check on the duration of the scenes, enabling them to pace the production to the climax described in the epilogue of the novel: Rogozhin becomes resigned to the hell that is in store for him, while Myshkin returns to the asylum in a worse state than when he left it and with little hope of recovery.

To indicate this, in the final moments Myshkin's speech breaks down into complete incoherence, while Rogozhin seems to regain his awareness, returns to reality and resolves to face his punishment. He sews money into the lining of his coat in preparation for his journey to Siberia, dresses himself for departure and finally opens the door wide. After the spectators were admitted, it had been locked as a symbol of the two men's complete isolation from the outside world. He is about to leave but returns for the crazed Prince. The play ends as together they leave the room slowly, wearily, at which point it is hard to tell whether they are still Myshkin and Rogozhin or the actors Nowicki and Radziwilowicz.

Even though there might have been no such thing as a typical performance, for obvious reasons certain themes were retained in each performance although they might occur in a different sequence. In addition there were some key fragments that remained constant in order to provide a structural skeleton within which the actors could work freely without losing the through line. Rogozhin's deliberations on the subject of religion, the exchanging of crucifixes, and the blessing bestowed by Rogozhin's mother on Myshkin were among these. So was Rogozhin's imaginary attempt to kill Myshkin, which (along the lines of psychodrama) might also turn into the murder of Nastasya, the sequence concerning Holbein's painting, and Rogozhin's complaints of the moral suffering Nastasya had caused him during their engagement. However, probably because of the need for such a structure to focus the performance, it was noticeable that in spite of the general rule of 'no blocking' the repetition of particular situations led to a certain mechanization in the way the performers interacted. Relatively few and generalized as they were, such moments brought about a lowering of the tension that was created during authentic innovatory explorations.

At the same time, even where the acting was at its most improvisational there was an inner consistency to the actors' performances. Between them, Jan Nowicki and Jerzy Radziwilowicz created characters almost totally in accord with Jung's typology of human character. Nowicki portrayed

Madness, love and death

Rogozhin as an extrovert in every behavioural trait and vocal inflection. Radziwilowicz, as Myshkin, represented the introvert — lost in himself, listening to inner voices, apparently cut off from his partner. Such an approach gives an expressive interpretation of Dostoyevsky's style that is in harmony with the most profound content of his work. Both protagonists complement each other, together they represent two sides of human nature: the dark is Rogozhin, the light Myshkin. In this respect, the basic concept of the production and the actors' portrayal of the characters was true to the spirit of novel, however much the performances might depart from the letter.

This dualism made contact between the actors harder to achieve, but in working against their natural tendency towards identification it raised the emotional tension of the performance. Indeed, the whole production was based on establishing a theatrical context that ran counter to normal acting impulses, and this in itself brought out the inherent thematic content in the dramatic material. The absolute freedom given to the actors demanded a full responsibility, which corresponded to the insight gained by Dostoyevsky's characters. Wajda acted as the inspirator and animator. Although the machinery could not have been set in motion without his experience and the influence of his personality, it was as if, having set the machine going, he left it to run on its own. Yet this abdication of his controlling function demonstrates his quality as a director in creating a perfect match between presentation and theme, subordinating his role to the requirements of the piece.

The Stary Teatr's production of *Nastasya Filippovna* was subsequently staged in various countries, and it was fascinating to see how far differences in context changed the performance — not only in the way new surroundings affected the psychological state of the actors, which was to be expected, but also in the way the response of the audience altered the overall meaning of the piece. This was most noticeable with audiences who had been exposed to Grotowski's theories and identified modern Polish theatre with the work of his Teatr Laboratorium. Although in some superficial respects the end result of this particular production was comparable, the confusion with Grotowski is misleading and leads to an under-valuing of Wajda's significance for contemporary theatre. As the critic Elzbieta Morawiec correctly pointed out,

> *Nastasya Filippovna* is not an imitation of Grotowski. Wajda used entirely different working methods, his ideas were based on quite different premises. When staging *Apocalypis cum Figuris* Grotowski rejected the conventional stage and also ruled out the concept of theatre as an institution devoted to the 'staging' of plays . . . whereas Wajda does not cut himself off from the institution of theatre. Moreover the risk of open rehearsals, jointly undertaken by Wajda and his actors, gave the theatre its own 'raison d'être'. The number of people in the audience was not limited by strict principles, as it is in Grotowski's theatre by his requirement that the audience should 'live through' the performance and be totally concentrated. Rather it was due simply to limitations of space

in the small venue at the Stary Teatr ... Finally, Grotowski's productions are performed by actors whom he intensively trains 'psycho/physically', whereas Wajda treats his actors in *Nastasya Filippovna* as professionally mature people. He questions neither their capability nor their method, confident of their sensibility and creative spontaneity. What, in that case, have these two diverse attitudes to theatre in common? First and foremost the fact that their composition is based on the juxtaposition of contrasts, and the use of polyphony. Secondly the rejection of the 'performance' [product] as the final and immutable outcome of rehearsals [process]. And thirdly, the principle of improvisation which outlines the text in the initial phase, thus forming a framework within which the actors have freedom in subsequent performances.[3]

Indeed, it was the elements which linked this production most closely to Grotowski's work that in the final assessment were least satisfactory. If the experiment's actual effect did not quite live up to the initial expectations, it was because of the contradiction between theatrical convention and total improvisation.

I think that everyone who took part in the experiment agrees. Even when based on a defined literary work with definite characters (as opposed to a proposed theme when the situation and characters are abstract and have no specified psychological characteristics) improvisation is difficult and risky, especially for a professional actor used to a very different task. In this sense it is doubtless a healthy shock, a cathartic professional experience. It is however an experience not worth repeating for itself. The approach can only be justified by its appropriateness to a specific type of dramatic material.

It must also be said that the public rehearsals were only an interesting 'one-off' experiment, and left much to be desired as an effective working method. The most interesting and memorable moments occurred during the private rehearsals rather than when the audience was present, while it was only when public rehearsals had been suspended that the final shape of the production crystallized.

To Wajda the lesson was clear: 'I had always thought there are many moments that require privacy. A rehearsal is certainly one of them. Up until now this had been no more than intuition, now I am certain of it. However it was worth rehearsing for twenty-seven evenings to find out for sure.'[4]

Wajda's two productions based on Dostoyevsky had explored diametrically opposed aspects of theatre. In *The Possessed* Wajda had mobilized a wealth of artistic means to produce an unrestrained visual spectacle that reproduced most of the numerous themes in the novel, finding a separate form of expression for each and not limiting himself to any established convention or style. By contrast, in his adaptation of *The Idiot* Wajda's aim was to impose a maximum of self-limitation, concentrating and condensing the various threads of the story, and expressing them in a consciously restrained and uniform theatrical style. Where *The Possessed* employed a compelling tempo to expand performance time to an epic scale, in *Nastasya Filippovna* time stood still and the expressive qualities seemed to be directed inwards. The point was not to present a series of events but to show the psychological effect of their consequences. Direct creation, incorporated in the principle of improvisation, replaced reproduction — and Wajda's intention was encapsulated by one review, which encouraged the public to 'Come and see how a whole world is created in one and a half hours by two actors.'[5]

Both lines of experiment merged in *Crime and Punishment*, the final production of Wajda's Dostoyevsky trilogy. In *The Possessed*, Wajda had begun with Camus' adaptation, which attempted to embrace the whole novel. Feeling that even so certain elements essential to the scenic structure were missing he was forced to make changes and enlarge upon it. In *Nastasya Filippovna* the text of *The Idiot* was cut and condensed into a two-hander, focussing — as through a lens — not so much on the theme, but on the spirit, atmosphere and sense of the novel. The stage version of *Crime and Punishment* was a kind of 'half-way house' between these two extremes.

None of Dostoyevsky novels makes light reading but *Crime and Punishment* is an exceptionally tough work. Its wide range of characters, plots and problems constitutes a rich mosaic of psychological, sociological and behavioural features. There have been many adaptations of this book and most adaptors have emphasized the many intricate secondary plots in order to illustrate the wealth and many-sidedness of the novel. Wajda's experience had shown the impracticality of attempting to transfer the entire contents of any Dostoyevsky novel onto the stage. Paradoxically, the more faithful to the novel the adaptor wishes to be, the more he must condense in order to embrace its entirety, cutting the many layers and dimensions that attracted him in the first place. However, Wajda believed a solution might be found in the theory voiced by the Russian expert on Dostoyevsky, Mikhail Bakhtin. In his book *The Problems of Dostoyevsky's Poetics*,[6] he maintains that Dostoyevsky's greatness lies in the polyphony of his works, which comes out most strongly in his method of narration through dialogue. Dostoyevsky hardly ever uses objective illustration, but introduces characters and situations through conversation. In this way he is able to present problems from several points of view as well as subjectively. This is the source of the sense of richness of experience and truth that we experience whilst reading Dostoyevsky's works, since we learn about each event independently through the eyes of the protagonists. It is this in particular which gives Dostoyevsky's work its dramatic potential, although not a single one of his works was actually written for the theatre.

Following this line Wajda focussed on the use of dialogue to reach the moral core of *Crime and Punishment*. This in itself obviously poses the question: What is the most vital and basic problem in this novel? Is it an indictment of nineteenth-century Russian society which produced Raskolnikov, or the psychological study of a murderer, or perhaps merely a 'thriller' about murder and detection? For Wajda twentieth-century events had decisively shifted its significance:

> Today I would interpret *Crime and Punishment* as a novel about the motives behind idealistic murder. I say 'today' because I am adapting the novel to create contemporary theatre and in so doing I have a responsibility towards the society I live in. Raskolnikov's article on the subject of crime and the way he chooses to interpret it to the Public Prosecutor Porfiry Piotrovitch is of the greatest significance to me. I know this kind of argument only too well: from the Nazi Concentration Camps to the most recent political murders. Bloodshed is acceptable if it is necessary (not even essential) to the general progress of mankind.[7]

In the Poland of late 1984, the social climate responsible for Raskolnikov's crime and the psychological character study had been transformed into a moral problem through Dostoyevsky's frequent return to themes from the Gospel. Biblical reference in *Crime and Punishment* is also a reference to the source of European morality, and its transcendental origins. In this interpretation (proposed by the Polish specialist on Dostoyevsky, Stanislaw Cat-Mackiewicz) murder is not merely a criminal offence but the crossing of a boundary that has not been set by man and may not be overstepped by him. Raskolnikov admits to his crime because in the course of his confrontation with Porfiry he realizes that he has sinned, that the theory he had created for his own justification is false. His crime is futile, since it proved nothing. He will seek redemption in subordinating himself to the moral principle he has violated, awaiting 'resurrection' from the moral 'grave' to which he has committed himself.

The main focus in Wajda's *Crime and Punishment* became the dialogue between three people: the murderer Raskolnikov, the prosecutor Porfiry Piotrovitch, and a young prostitute named Sonya. Undoubtedly the most important is the dialogue between Raskolnikov and Porfiry, a refined intellectual game where logic wrestles with utopian ideas. But this is both complemented and counterpointed by the dialogue with Sonya, the one person to whom Raskolnikov speaks openly. This dialectic defines the central issue: is there any moral justification for killing a man? Sonya represents a straightforward, natural morality which has its deep roots in religion. There is even a suggestion that the simplicity and singlemindedness of her ethical outlook makes a stronger impression on Raskolnikov than Porfiry's logic. Wajda's stress on the moral theme of the story meant leaving aside the social background and a whole gallery of picturesque figures like Swidrygaylov and Marmieladov. Only a few minor characters, whose appearance renders the

Madness, love and death

main action clearer, were retained. Following the approach set in his previous Dostoyevsky production Wajda concentrated the entire material of the novel onto this trio, searching out the spirit of the work, synthetically condensing it in contrast to merely producing a paraphrase of the story.

Having learnt from his production of *Nastasya Filippovna* that the intimacy created by proximity alone can intensify the dramatic experience, Wajda presented *Crime and Punishment* in 'close-up' to the audience. This not only denied his actors any possibility of pretence, but corresponded physically to the narrow focus of his interpretation.

In the first version of *Crime and Punishment* an audience of about 80 people sat on the stage of the Stary Teatr, where the action took place. Wajda felt this confined space, in which people were 'packed together', produced the desired effect. The play consisted of two parts. In the first, the audience was seated on the proscenium facing the back of the stage, and in the second their seats were moved to face the auditorium, which was curtained off. Changing the angle of vision reinforced Wajda's concept of the 'audience as witnesses'. For the final scene in Siberia, where Raskolnikov is living out his sentence, the curtain separating the audience from the auditorium opened: white smoke hovering over the comparatively large space of the auditorium suggested the boundless immensity of the Siberian landscape.

However, this seating arrangement had to be abandoned after the first few performances due to technical difficulties. Re-seating the audience made the interval too long, and since only a maximum of 100 people could watch the play, the 600-seat auditorium was being wasted for the sake of a single scene. Subsequently, the production was moved to the venue used for *Nastasya Filippovna*. Here the audience remained seated in the same place throughout, but the physical intimacy was enhanced. In some sequences the actors were a mere metre or two away from people sitting in the first row, separated only by a wooden barrier. To compensate for the loss of the shift in perspective, the already confined area was divided into even smaller spaces by partially glazed partitions. Some scenes were therefore watched by the audience through dust-covered panes of glass, producing the impression that they were spying on strangers in private and even intimate situations. That feeling of voyeurism, of 'real life' taking place before the audience's eyes, was intensified by Krystyna Zachwatowicz's setting, which was limited to those shabby partitions dividing the area into several rooms. The dilapidated furniture, as well as the costumes and props, were meticulously in period, and there was no sign of theatrical convention. On the contrary, these 'interiors' were designed for maximum realism and authenticity. With the audience so close, the least falsification or imitation would not only be noticed but would destroy the atmosphere.

The first half of the play takes place in the Public Prosecutor's apartment.

29 *Crime and Punishment*, Cracow 1984. General view of the set. Raskolnikov (Jerzy Radziwilowicz, centre) enters Porfiry's apartment (Porfiry: Jerzy Stuhr). (Razumichin, on the right: Krzysztof Globisz.)

Through the dusty window-panes the audience could see into his study, with its desk and heavy armchairs, and also into his little drawing-room where there is evidence of a party having taken place on the previous night. In the second half the set represents Sonya's modest apartment and Raskolnikov's even shabbier room. Downstage, alongside the barrier separating the audience from the 'acting area', a long glass-topped display cabinet exhibits the incriminating evidence: a bloody axe, precious objects stolen from the murdered pawnbroker, documents . . . a morbid display, bearing witness to the fact that the murder has already been committed and indicating that our interest is now focussed on its consequences. The lighting, provided by the various lamps that light the different rooms, contributed to the authenticity of the set design, with fast light-changes being used to give the production its rhythm and steer the audience's attention.

Madness, love and death

30 *Crime and Punishment*, Cracow 1984. Final scene: view of Siberia.

The action begins as Raskolnikov comes to Porfiry's apartment, not yet as the suspect, but as a friend. The subtle psychological game between them commences. We get to know the Public Prosecutor informally at home, after an all-night party: he is dishevelled, slovenly, and continuously complaining of a headache; he hardly appears much of an adversary. Raskolnikov looks unconcerned. Although burdened with the awareness of his crime, he is still confident in the viability of his theory. The action proper begins with Porfiry's mention of Raskolnikov's article on the subject of crime. While developing his theory of crime motivated by idealism, the student's sudden animation and emotional tension reveal that something lies hidden in the depth of his being. Porfiry watches him intently, from time to time throwing in a captious remark or pinning him down with an unexpected question. He is not, after all, an insignificant, drunken official but a formidable opponent of sharp intellect. Raskolnikov perceives this: with their first conversation, not yet linked directly with the murder of the old pawnbroker, their confrontation is already established.

In this production the inevitability of Raskolnikov's fate was accentuated not as a consequence of the murder he has committed, but because of moral necessity as the Public Prosecutor's role changes. Rather than being merely a clever lawyer who forces the suspect to admit his crime, he takes on the attributes of a confessor, beckoning the sinner away from a life of crime. His aim is that the other man himself may realize and understand his error.

31 *Crime and Punishment*, Cracow 1984. Porfiry (Jerzy Stuhr) interrogates Raskolnikov (Jerzy Radziwilowicz).

Their relationship becomes so significant in Wajda's production because Raskolnikov does not confess through fear of punishment, but because he realizes that punishment must come so that the world may regain its lost equilibrium. Raskolnikov and Porfiry are not just a criminal and a policeman, not just the hunter and the hunted, but two human beings living through a drama of consciousness.

We feel that Porfiry does not fight against Raskolnikov but for him and consequently for himself. He has no desire to destroy the man. On the contrary he wants to save him, and in so doing give his own life a deeper meaning. It is this that motivates the fascinating change of personality in Porfiry from a squalid little police official into a thinking, caring man. Nevertheless he cannot totally rid himself of his professional traits as a court official, and the element of game-playing is ever-present, even though at

Madness, love and death 87

32 *Crime and Punishment*, Cracow 1984. Reading of the Bible.
Raskolnikov (Jerzy Radziwilowicz), seated at the table, listens to the child,
while Sonya (Barbara Grabowska-Oliva) stays back to the left.

times it is extremely refined and subtle. The way the Prosecutor belittles himself in the eyes of Raskolnikov, his manifestations of typical Russian humility and affected friendship, are theatrical: a play within the play. The actor is playing a character who is himself playing a part.

The character of Sonya, less colourful by comparison, serves to express what is left unsaid in the scenes between Porfiry and Raskolnikov. To some degree Wajda's decision not to interpret the social significance of *Crime and Punishment* limits Sonya's character, since it is in this context that she is most clearly defined in the novel. A passive partner to Raskolnikov, nevertheless it is she who is the link between the murderer denying Christian morality and the Gospel. In one of the most moving scenes in the play Raskolnikov asks Sonya to read him the story of the 'Raising of Lazarus' from the Bible. She finds the passage but, held back by her own transgressions, cannot bring herself to read it. It is Sonya's younger sister who finally reads the Gospel story. The symbolism is implicit: only an innocent child has the right to voice what Raskolnikov denies and Sonya feels unworthy of. However at the end of the play, in Siberia, it is Sonya herself who reads Raskolnikov the same passage from the Gospel. The parallel not only underlines the recurring motif of the play, but serves to measure the profound change that has taken place in the characters.

The agony of Raskolnikov's inner struggle with, as Kant put it, 'the moral law within me', which he sought to deny in vain even though he had been capable of double murder, was brilliantly perceived. In Jerzy Radziwilowicz's interpretation Raskolnikov's pathological anxiety seemed similar to the insanity of Prince Myshkin, the role he had played in *Nastasya Filippovna*, although a more extrovert rendering. By contrast the most striking element in Jerzy Stuhr's performance as Porfiry Piotrovitch, the Public Prosecutor, was his expressive interpretation of the character's external physical traits: a nervous giggle, hyperactivity and sudden changes of mood. He succeeded in portraying a character at once repulsive and fascinating. In the way they presented strongly delineated personalities both actors became exponents of what could be described as one of the most interesting features of Andrzej Wajda's theatre: the psychological and moral duality, even ambiguity, of dramatic characters; the transformation of a human being in his search for truth. It is here that the dramatic explorations of the director converge with Dostoyevsky's most profound philosophy as an artist, which helps to explain Wajda's continuing fascination with the Russian writer.

The actors were unable to 'cheat' by using 'technique', due to the extreme proximity of the audience. Jerzy Radziwilowicz, a sensitive perfectionist, had starred in Wajda's films *Man of Marble* and *Man of Iron*, as well as taking the part of Prince Myshkin in *Nastasya Filippovna*. Jerzy Stuhr, one of the most versatile actors in Poland, had already appeared in many of Wajda's productions, from the title role of *Hamlet* and Wysocki in *November Night* to AA in *The Emigrants*, as well as taking over as Verkhovensky in *The Possessed*. The fact that both were experienced not only in Wajda's working methods, but also in the interpretation of Dostoyevsky's characters contributed to their unique performances, in which they were able almost totally to identify with their characters. In order to submerge the actor's personality in that of the character portrayed, talent and technique are not enough; the actor must rid himself of all inhibitions in a way analogous to the process undergone by the figures in the play. At one moment Raskolnikov says: 'Let him who has a conscience suffer; that will be his punishment.' Those words were the key to Wajda's production. He showed suffering that springs from the moral

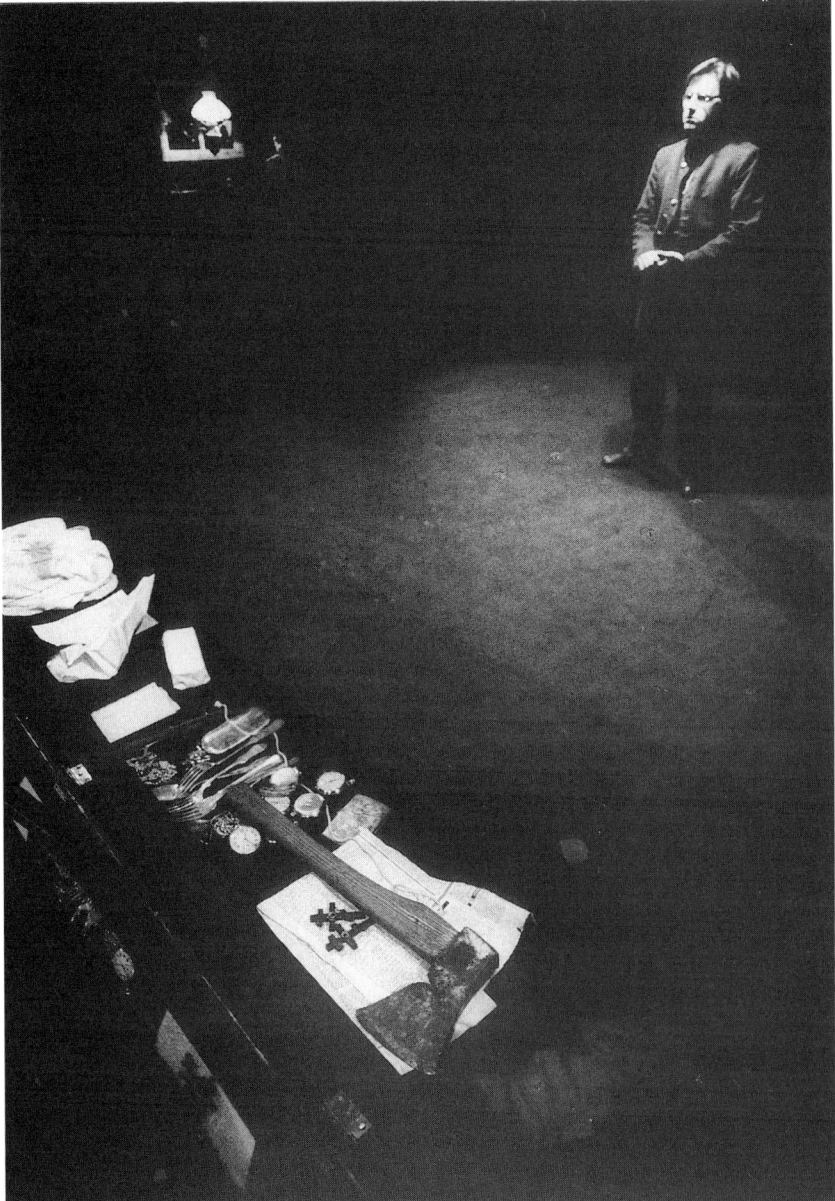

33 *Crime and Punishment*, Cracow 1984. Raskolnikov's confession. In the foreground, display of the material evidence of the crime. Raskolnikov (Jerzy Radziwilowicz) stays in the background.

consciousness of the individual. The play's message is that morality springs from a source outside and above humanity, and that consequently crime cannot be justified, either intellectually or idealistically. At that point in Poland (winter 1984–5), this had a highly contemporary and political significance.

At the same time presentation and content overlapped so completely that the dominant impression left by the production was a communion with truth. This was achieved not only by the authenticity of the set design or the feeling of witnessing actual events, but also by acting that bordered on psychological exhibitionism. This gave an at times embarrassing element to the superficially neutral part of witnesses that the audience was given. In addition they were implicitly asked to reach a verdict. During the penultimate scene when Raskolnikov relates his crime, he takes the exhibits out of the showcase one by one. The court official takes them from him and shows them to the audience so that they may inspect them closely, as though they were a jury. The nature of Raskolnikov's crime becomes apparent: calculating, rationalized, anything but the work of a sick mind. Our world is well acquainted with 'ideological crime', not only from the pages of Dostoyevsky's novel and the theatre, but from daily experience – and the role imposed on the audience developed the political point, which was reinforced by the authenticity of the performance without the parallel being made explicit.

In *The Possessed*, despite the monumental staging, the most important themes were contained in the dialogue between Verkhovensky and Stavrogin. In *Nastasya Filippovna* Prince Myshkin and Rogozhin 'created a world', as it were, through their improvised dialogue. In *Crime and Punishment* the dialogue between the Public Prosecutor and the criminal became a quest for the source and meaning of morality. Basically this 'dialogue' remained the same throughout the trilogy. It encapsulated the 'drama of consciousness' in our times, which Dostoyevsky foresaw so perceptively.

6 A reckoning with the past: *Conversations with the Executioner* and *As the Days Pass, As the Years Pass*

During the seven years that separated the production of *Nastasya Filippovna* from that of *Crime and Punishment*, Wajda staged productions as diverse as *Conversations with the Executioner* (1977), *As the Days Pass, As the Years Pass* (1978) and the Cracow *Hamlet* (1981). The first two have one thing in common: both cast a retrospective glance at, and settle an account with, the past, although they differed widely in style. *As the Days Pass, As the Years Pass* was very long, diversified in focus and eclectic in its use of historical, sociological and cultural sources. *Conversations with the Executioner*, on the other hand, was a straightforward documentary staged with ascetic restraint. The director's motivation in treating the literary material in each case, however, was the same: to make a personal judgement on the past.

The book on which the production of *Conversations with the Executioner* was based came about in unusual and moving circumstances that were the result of the existence of two diverse political factions during the Second World War in Poland, both dedicated to fighting the Nazi Occupation by means of an underground army. However, this was their only common cause. The AK, the Home Army, headed by an *émigré* government based in London, was democratic, pro-Western and wanted a return to the pre-war status quo in Poland. The AL, the People's Army, supported by Moscow, was fighting for a Communist government in Poland. When Soviet troops entered Poland, members of the Home Army were treated as enemies in much the same way as the Nazis. Wajda had already dealt with the tragic dilemmas of those times in the films *Ashes and Diamonds* and above all *Canal*, where the Russians are shown holding back their assault while the Home Army is massacred by the Germans. It is a matter of historical record that the AK were encouraged to start the Warsaw Uprising as the Russians approached the city; but instead of aiding the insurgents, the Soviet Army halted until their potential opposition had been wiped out.

As soon as the Second World War ended the new Polish authorities began to arrest the remaining officers of the Home Army, ignoring their heroic resistance against the Germans. Amongst those arrested was Kazimierz Moczarski, a high-ranking officer who was subsequently sentenced to death for treason. While awaiting execution Moczarski was imprisoned in the same cell as a Nazi war criminal, the general of the SS who had been in command of the Police, Jurgen Stroop. This man, had, among other things, been responsible for the bloody liquidation of the Warsaw ghetto. In short, a Polish anti-fascist, and member of the Underground Army, found himself sharing a cell with his deadly enemy, a man whom not so long ago he had himself been planning to assassinate. Day and night for many months, he was confined in a tiny space with one of Hitler's bloodiest butchers. What is more, he was treated as an equal criminal.

Not having much choice, Moczarski decided to take advantage of the situation. In view of his forced cohabitation with Stroop, he decided to get to know the man and endeavour to understand him. From these lengthy 'conversations with the executioner' evolved a fascinating and harrowing book. Eventually, when policy changed, he was released, rehabilitated, and his account was finally published.

The facts that Moczarski relates are history. But their interpretation – as seen by Stroop, the uniformed murderer, a man whose sense of morality had undergone a pathological regression and whose fanatical sense of duty to the Führer superseded his conscience – forms a stunning document.

Unlike in *Ashes and Diamonds*, the historical details of the fight against fascism or the ideologically motivated betrayal of the Polish resistance were of secondary importance to Wajda here. His professional interest in this material centred on its attempt to understand how fascism could have led to such moral and psychological depravity. How any ideology could produce people like Jurgen Stroop, a man who murdered thousands yet could speak tenderly about children, a man who was insensitive to the perpetration of the Holocaust yet would happily converse about the subtleties of fine cuisine. This psychological and moral investigation, with a significance reaching beyond the merely historical, was what attracted Wajda to make a stage adaptation of the book.

The production in the Studio of the Teatr Powszechny in Warsaw, in 1977, began with a characteristic prologue: Zygmunt Hübner as Moczarski, dressed in an ordinary suit and clutching a bunch of flowers, sat on a simple chair in the glare of stage lighting. An author publicizing his book at an open meeting with his readers, he responded to the customary questions from the audience. These were posed by actors planted in the auditorium and established the historical context which gave rise to the book in the first place. But the prologue was also important from a theatrical point of view: it created 'distance', removing theatrical illusion from the production and giving the performance the features of an intellectual discussion.

Only after this did we enter the prison cell. Its reconstruction by Wajda and his designer Alan Starski was highly naturalistic: a tiny gloomy room with wooden beds, a small barred window and a steel door directly opposite

A reckoning with the past

34 *Conversations with the Executioner*, Warsaw 1977. Realistic picture of life in prison: Schielke (Kazimierz Kaczor), Moczarski (Zygmunt Hübner) and Stroop (Stanislaw Zaczyk).

the audience. It gave the actual feel of prison existence, and the stifling, claustrophobic effect of the atmosphere was enhanced by the lighting and an extraordinarily realistic range of acoustic effects re-creating sounds typical of a prison building.

A series of scenes depicting prison life follows the prologue: at first Stroop shares a cell with another German, Schielke. Then Moczarski arrives. Their initial confrontation gives place to reluctant contact, and later to regular conversations. All the while the fact that this takes place in prison is stressed by the rhythm of passing days, nights and months, the recurring interrogations and walks in the prison yard. The precision and terseness of the stage effects was striking — instead of depicting physical torture in detail, a short black-out, a single terrible cry, then the lights would come on to show

Moczarski being dragged back to his cell by silent Polish guards. The paradoxical image of two Nazis helping a Pole after his brutal interrogation by fellow Poles was a bitter historical comment. In turn, a provocative scene in which the defeated Nazi general, the war criminal awaiting execution, entertained his cellmates by singing the praises of life in the German army whilst energetically performing the goose step, vividly encapsulated the deep and unacknowledged workings of the human psyche.

As in the case of Mrozek's *The Emigrants* one might speculate on the seemingly insignificant role of the director in a play where the spoken word is the vital ingredient, and the 'acting' is limited by scenic conditions that repress the director's imagination. However, it is obvious from these two productions that Wajda does not see the director's role as setting the scenes and blocking the moves, or devising the most effective lighting and technical devices. He sees it as presenting, with maximum clarity, the polemical aspect of the drama, be it a fictional work or, as in the case of *Conversations with the Executioner*, one based solely on historical events. In this production there were long moments when the actors merely sat and talked. Yet the dramatic content of their facial expressions during conversation was more expressive than any 'theatrical effect'.

The documentary treatment excluded all striking dramaturgical statements and deliberately avoided any effective climax or moral. There was, however, one point made in a strictly theatrical sense. Once the play was over, a beam of light searched out the chair that Moczarski sat on in the prologue, now empty but for the bunch of flowers. Emotionally powerful precisely because of its simplicity and restraint, this final gesture paid silent tribute to all those who had fought the oppression, violence and brutality that we describe with the word 'fascism', everything that in its human embodiment is so clearly brought out in *Conversations with the Executioner*.

A few years ago on my return from a trip abroad, I told Wajda of a theatrical production by Robert Wilson entitled *The Life and Times of Joseph Stalin* that I had seen in Copenhagen, which lasted twelve hours. Commencing at eight in the evening, it went on until eight in the morning. My description stressed one particular aspect that had intrigued me most – the role that the temporal process played in the production: when, as it were, time took on a meaning in its own right, which in turn led to the authentication of whatever was taking place on stage. The world as portrayed on the stage – autonomous, symbolist, fragmentary – became the rightful equal of the world of reality, with the result that the moment of confrontation between those two worlds, on leaving the theatre, became a strange and unforgettable experience. Wajda showed considerable interest in the idea, and it became the seed of his production *As the Days Pass, As the Years Pass*, which was an attempt to come to grips with the problem of time in the theatre.

This production comprised three parts, each lasting as long as a full-length play. Taking about seven hours from start to finish, it was either performed on three consecutive nights or continuously, lasting into the early hours, and the duration of the performance itself had a specific thematic function. Produced by Wajda in the Stary Teatr in Cracow, it had much in common with the structure of a television serial.[1] The themes of the various episodes intermeshed, yet each could be treated as a separate narrative and a single one usually formed the main subject for each episode. These separate themes in themselves retained an intimate character, but their sum-total rendered a vast panorama which was truly epic in scope. Wajda's previous productions had tended to concentrate exclusively on either epic breadth or intimacy, achieving the extreme of one quality at the expense of the other. *As the Days Pass, As the Years Pass* was an attempt to synthesize the two contrasting directions in his work: the monumental and the psychological.

The scenario joined together fragments from a number of Polish literary works — some well known, others almost completely forgotten — written in the years between the close of the nineteenth century and the First World War. The action took place in Cracow, and spanned the whole period during which the works had been written. The common thread binding these fragments together was the family ties and social connections extrapolated between the protagonists in each episode, whose names and life histories were changed to fit them into two middle-class families: the Chominski family, featured in a little-known Polish drama by Kiesielewski, and the Dulski family from the play *Mrs Dulska's Morality* by Gabriela Zapolska,[2] the most familiar example of the 'critical realism' period in Polish drama. The resulting 'theatrical novel' was the saga of these typical families, whose members represent personalities and attitudes formed by the Cracow environment and in turn forming the social milieu and particular atmosphere of that historic town. Cracow itself — the cultural architecture and the human geography — became the main subject of Wajda's production.

In addition the script placed authentic writers and painters closely linked with the town alongside the fictitious characters. Thus the popular comedy writer Michal Balucki appears on the stage with figures from his own works, as does his literary antagonist Stanislaw Przybyszewski (the father of the author of *The Danton Affair*, Stanislawa Przybyszewska). They are joined by other writers and painters, presented as if brought to life, not in their own art, but in the imagination of different authors. The effect was not only a kind of 'literary game'. It also served as a persuasive way of presenting contemporary ideas, so that literature was seen to be nurtured by life and inextricably

35 *As the Days Pass, As the Years Pass*, Cracow 1978.
'Family photograph' – the final scene of the second act.

intertwined with it; and in this mixture of fact with fiction the scenario itself mirrored the kind of literature from which its episodes derived: mainly realistic in style, but conceptually on the borderline between modern symbolism and naturalism. Such a technique lent itself particularly well to the portrayal of a vast panorama embracing the life of a city through its inhabitants, allowing the imagination of a director free play, as well as giving the entire company of the Stary Teatr the opportunity to create a gallery of colourful characters in various personifications as a result of the time span.

The action begins in 1874 and ends with the outbreak of the First World War in 1914, on the day the Polish Legions set out from Cracow to carry the Polish flag into the Great War. By the last decades of the nineteenth century traditions of struggle for political independence were regaining their vitality beneath the surface mood of accommodation to the status quo, which was underpinned by social and cultural conservatism. The younger generation represented a new radical patriotism. Much the same happened in the sphere of culture as in politics. Authors as varied as Wyspianski, Balucki and Przybyszewski were all writing during this period, in which Przybyszewski's colourful, yet sterile, modernistic decadence coexisted with the first staging

A reckoning with the past

of *The Wedding* and the first publication of *November Night*. It was a time of change, of conflicting trends and ever more violent clashes between 'old' and 'new'.

In the homes of the two families the various topical conflicts take the form of family disputes. The conservatism of the older generation provokes resistance and rebellion in the young – yet 'as the years pass' they also age, and many of them fail to remain loyal to their youthful ideals. Wajda's portrayal emphasized this process: showing the oppression and the demoralization of individuals through the pressure of family, tradition and even the physical surroundings, perhaps above all through their own city, for this play, despite its positive portrayal of the great cultural centre that has nurtured so much of the Polish intelligentsia, did not sentimentalize it. Wajda's production was also an indictment, exposing the social milieu as the source of the same symptoms of intellectual and spiritual stagnation that Wyspianski satirized in *The Wedding*. Like so much of Wajda's work the approach explored a dialectic of opposites, but on a broader canvas than ever before – the destructive traits together with those that still form the basis of the town's individuality and originality today; social criticism together with some strongly patriotic themes; artistic creation and political action; revolution and repression. It embraced almost all the themes of Wajda's work to this point, documenting the change of awareness of Polish society on the eve of the short-lived national independence which came in 1918.

The kind of dramatic material to which Wajda turned his attention in this production had played a large part in the formation of a national literary and theatrical culture for Poland, and its recovery for the stage held an implicit political point. The fact that so much of this work had been discarded in the contemporary era was taken to indicate the same sort of compromising accommodation against which the younger generations within the play rebelled. Its revival as such implied a reawakening of the national consciousness that this drama incorporated. At the same time other fragments of *As the Days Pass, As the Years Pass* were 'dug up' from total obscurity to portray a reactionary outlook or the negative impact of the cultural environment, and these were presented perversely or in the form of pastiche. The aim here could be compared to Peter Stein's technique of searching out and staging forgotten French farces, in order to evaluate modern bourgeois society.

It is important to note that the middle-class tradition is more colourful, and plays a more important role, in the cultures of Germany and other Western European countries than in Poland where the country's culture is drawn mainly from an upper-class, courtly and aristocratic heritage. Thus Wajda's portrayal of the part played by the middle classes in Polish history was, in itself, a novel idea breaking with accepted stereotypes.

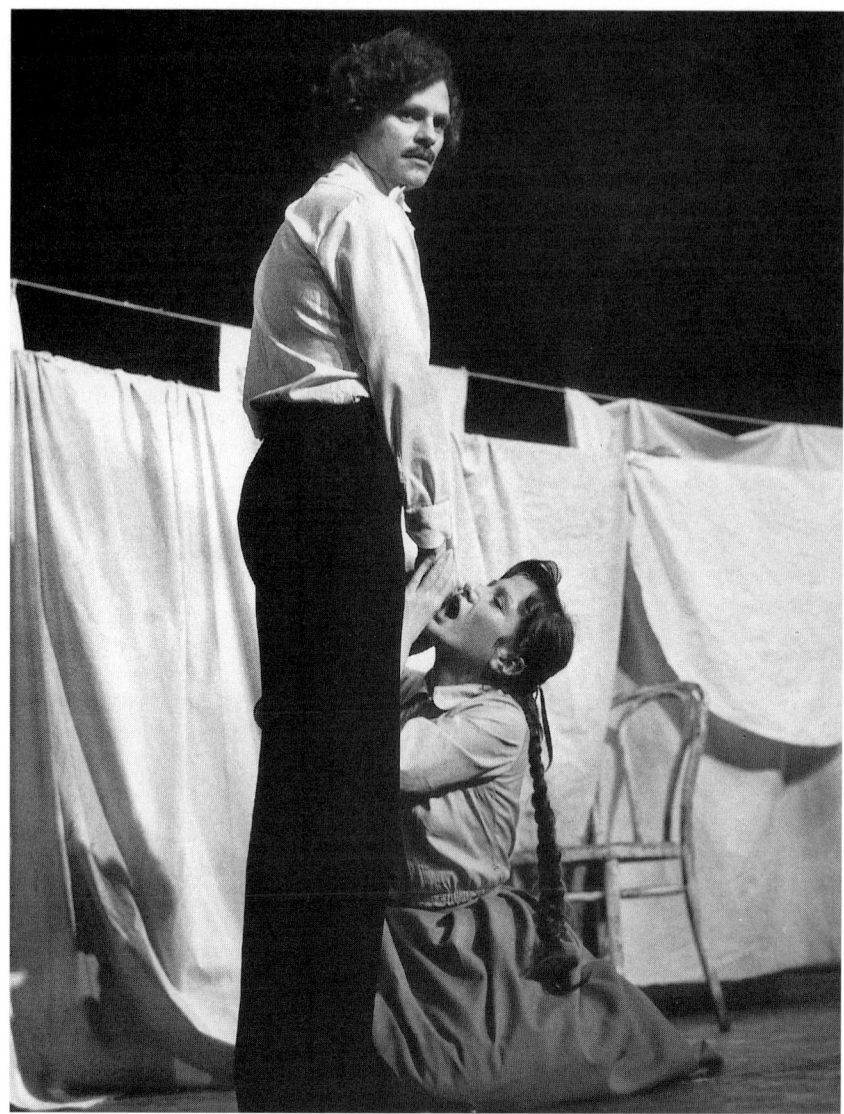

36 *As the Days Pass, As the Years Pass*, Cracow 1978. Sequence from naturalistic theatre. Young artist Relski (Mieczylaw Grabka) and poor servant girl Zosia (Ewa Kolasinska).

Wajda's monumental seven-hour spectacle was both a family chronicle and a wide canvas depicting community life and customs. Its solid, realistic form was a far cry from the formal experimentation of *Nastasya Filippovna* and *Crime and Punishment* or the explosive vision of *The Possessed* and *November*

37 *As the Days Pass, As the Years Pass*, Cracow 1978. Triumphant nouveau-riche Mrs Dulska (Anna Polony, right) forcing her own sister (Izabela Olszewska) to leave an apartment.

Night. Yet despite the stylistic limitations of realism the staging was full of wit and satirical elements, characterized by inventive directorial ideas bordering on pastiche. For instance, a young, emancipated Cracovienne, returning from an exhibition where she has seen a notorious picture depicting a naked woman riding a galloping horse (Podkowinski's painting entitled *Frenzy*, which caused an artistic scandal at the time), becomes almost frenzied herself as she tries to describe the painting to her family. Hardly realizing what she was doing, she clambers onto the shoulders of one of the servants in order to convey the pose of the heroine to the horrified onlookers. Although such an exaggerated approach imposed a certain distance and reserve in the treat-

38 *As the Days Pass, As the Years Pass*, Cracow 1978. Family portrait of the Dulskis.

ment of the material, Wajda also occasionally resorted to poignancy and pathos. Like an artist painting a huge family portrait he filled the stage with vivid, expressive characters, whose lives were depicted with great panache, against a minutely detailed background, composed of social conventions and the changing fashions of the time.

The most important 'protagonist' in this monumental production seemed to be Time itself. Wajda had already experimented with the perception of the temporal process in *Nastasya Filippovna*, although his aim in that production was to make time stand still in Rogozhin's sultry apartment, to show the frustrated attempts of people trying to put the clock back, nostalgically pursuing vanished time. Here the intention was the opposite: to show the flux

A reckoning with the past

of time, not time present; the thrust towards the future rather than a vain attempt to relive an irretrievable past. The very title encapsulated the idea behind the production: it conveys the effect of Time, all-powerful and ever-present, on the people, on the city and on history. People age, then die, while others are born to experience the crests and depths of life in their turn. History presses forward, changing society, declaring wars and raising up new countries, but the city remains unchanged, emanating the energy that creates its unique atmosphere. Thus the exceptional length of the production as such had thematic significance: it is a necessity for the audience to experience the passing of time at first hand. The spectators' weariness, as the play carries on into the night, a direct consequence of time passing, makes them more aware of the same process taking place on stage.

There was also an obvious significance in the choice of the Stary Teatr in Cracow for performing this production. Just as the town has taken a specific part in Polish history and culture, so the theatre plays an important role in Polish artistic life. The Stary Teatr itself not only symbolizes the endurance of tradition but is closely associated with progressive and innovatory dramaturgical trends, while through the centuries Poland's most bourgeois and conservative town has been the birthplace of new talent and ideas. It was here, surrounded by the solid base of traditional values — perhaps in protest and by contrast — that Polish theatrical reformers such as Wyspianski, Swinarski and Wajda found the right conditions for their work. In a sense Wajda can be seen as pitting his strength against the city of his youth, with its genius, its passion and its weighty heritage. He assessed it, and paid his tribute.

7 Towards a theatre of politics: *Hamlet*, *Antigone*, and *Easter Vigil*

As the introduction has already indicated, significant parallels, in form and above all in intellectual content, can be found between Andrzej Wajda's film and theatre work. It is not just a matter of stylistic cross-influence, nor of the handling and developing of similar plots, as in the screen and theatre versions of *The Wedding* or *The Danton Affair*, but of a deeper and more general relationship. *Conversations with the Executioner*, for instance, shares the same theme with the film of *Landscape after a Battle* (1970), which exposes with terrifying bitterness the moral effects of war. In turn the panoramic portrayal of an epoch as seen in *As the Days Pass, As the Years Pass* could be compared to *The Promised Land*, (1974), an epic film on a similar subject, while its psychological aspect has a direct relationship to *The Young Ladies of Wilko* (1979), a film devoted to the vain pursuit of lost youth. These similarities are obvious – although not always planned – and testify to the complementary nature of Andrzej Wajda's film and theatre work, when seen as an organic whole.

Wajda made two films in 1976 and 1981 which occupy a special place in his artistic achievement, *Man of Marble* and *Man of Iron*. These not only provide a dramatic summary of Polish contemporary history but hold an important place in European political cinema. That they also marked a return to Wajda's creative source, for he began his career with films on political themes, was not so much an indication of personal choice as the result of the situation in Poland at the time. He made a similar 'return' to political ideas in the theatre: first, to some extent, in *Hamlet* (1981), and subsequently, on a greater scale, in *Antigone* (1984).

The general conception behind *Hamlet* and its flaws have already been mentioned. Wajda's idea was to 'humanize' Hamlet through basing his portrayal on the 'Everyman' tradition. At the same time, by not relinquishing his monumental, stylized staging, he created a paradox which had a detrimental effect on the tempo and expressiveness of the production as well as on audience reaction. At first sight it might seem strange to include this production in a category of political theatre. However Wajda deliberately emphasized the political nature of the conflict between Hamlet and Claudius. The theme of personal revenge, the son's duty to avenge his father's death, was relegated to the background, while the conflict between the individual and authority, represented by the King and his court, became the primary

Towards a theatre of politics 103

issue. Claudius and Polonius stand for 'reasons of state', which contrast with the 'moral reasons' existing in the mind of the individual, Hamlet. Free use is made of all forms of manipulation, and Ophelia herself becomes no more than a pawn in the political game. Hamlet's indecision is transformed into the dilemma of a man enmeshed in a political situation and compelled to adopt a definite stance in a conflict which transcends the individual. In the same way the final scene, the arrival of Fortinbras, depicted as a soldier carrying out simple, arbitrary decisions, becomes the resolution of the political problem.

This theme of the individual's battle against authority, together with the conflict between personal morality and political 'necessity', was fully expounded only in *Antigone*. Wajda began work on Sophocles' tragedy in specific circumstances – martial law had been declared in Poland and he interpreted the play in this context. A politically updated version of *Antigone* had originally been conceived several years earlier, when Wajda discussed the idea of setting the action in modern Lebanon. In the late 1970s, as he told me, his intention was to show the play's age-old moral dilemma through the tragic situation of the Lebanese nation. Nobody could then foresee that this concept would be realized in different yet equally dramatic historical circumstances, of much greater personal significance to the director – and the genesis of the production is relevant primarily as an indication that its staging in 1984 was not a sudden impulse, even less opportunism, but emerged from considerations reaching deeper than martial law in Poland.

The words 'As long as I live I will cry out – No' from *Antigone* by Czeslaw Milosz, reprinted in the programme, served as a slogan for Wajda's production. In this poem, written in 1949, Milosz (the winner of the Nobel prize for literature in 1980 and a strong supporter of the Solidarity Movement) reasons in a similar way to Wajda: Antigone's protest is acknowledged as the archetype of revolutionary consciousness in twentieth-century man who is unwilling to accept the triumph of evil. The programme also provided a commentary on the production in the form of photographs from the international exhibition *Photo-Journalism 1977*, which depicted scenes of violence in various corners of the world today. Even before the play had begun a member of the audience, seated in his chair with the programme in his hand, would be in no doubt as to what the director and actors wished to convey to him.

Introducing modern costumes and contemporary theatre technique, Wajda placed the Greek tragedy in a 'living' cultural context, at the same time aiming it at a spectator emotionally conditioned to appreciate this specific plot by external events. The fact that the play was performed for such a clearly defined recipient was what made the production so controversial. Accepted unquestioningly by some, it was as decisively rejected by others,

39 *Antigone*, Cracow 1984. Chorus dressed as contemporary military commandos.

so that the public response to the play could almost be called a continuation of it, transferred, as it were, to the contemporary scene. As such the idea of transposing *Antigone* from classical antiquity to the most topical present day was not merely a formal device but became a 'touchstone' for the political and moral attitudes of a community involved in a specific psychological and political situation. Producing Sophocles' drama in this way Wajda did not so much update it as give it universal validity. In his own words:

> I chose that play because I thought it was currently most appropriate. But in order to ensure that the public might follow my interpretation and understand what I had to say, I had to find a more modern presentation, to update the costumes and design. I had to suggest to the spectator, in as many ways as possible, that he was not merely watching the revival of a Greek tragedy that bore some relevance to the present. My aim was that the audience should live through it as passionately as, no doubt, the original Greek audience did when the play was performed in the ancient amphitheatre.[1]

Towards a theatre of politics

The public reception of Wajda's *Antigone*, seen through the prism of contradictory reviews, confirmed the success of this approach in radicalizing the audience: the reactions of the critics and public corresponded to their political orientation. This is illustrated by two reviews, one in the government periodical *Polityka*, expressing the official view, and the other in the Catholic paper *Tygodnik Powszechny*, which is the closest thing to an organ of legal opposition possible in Poland. The two critics from opposite extremes of the political spectrum, watching the same play, apparently saw entirely different things. Even descriptions of the first-night audience's reaction were totally at variance. The critic for the *Tygodnik Powszechny* wrote: 'The majority of the audience on the first night of *Antigone* at the Stary Teatr felt that they were participating in a significant event which could herald the beginning of a new era in our theatre, restoring its lost standing and prestige.'[2] The review of *Polityka* read as follows: 'The public attending the first night at the Stary Teatr was totally disorientated. Some people stood up and applauded loudly, others remained seated and clapped politely, whilst others just whistled. This lasted for a moment, then came to an abrupt end, and the audience hurried to get their coats.'[3]

In fact the two critics did not agree on a single point, not merely in their evaluation of the play, which would be understandable, but in their description and interpretation of the production itself.

Polityka:

On stage we find a plastic palace that occupied the whole of the upper frame of the stage ... below, amidst metal scaffolding supporting the palace, the action takes place. The lights dim, and the stage fills with clouds of smoke. Commandos wearing combat fatigues appear and move forwards in closed ranks. They talk of the last battle, of victory and the satisfaction of victorious soldiers. They are in a joyous mood but their joy is to be short-lived, for it will be the cause of tears, so it is rather the harbinger of tragedy than the herald of peace. Antigone appears among the soldiers; sad, thin, her lips tightly pursed.[4]

Tygodnik Powszechny:

Wajda's royal palace is made of glass and steel ... on the upper storey in the semi-darkness the outline of a large, empty desk can be seen through the glass wall ... The play has a cyclical struture. It begins and ends with the Chorus. In the prologue it appears as soldiers in full battle dress, in the epilogue as workers dressed in grey quilted jackets and white protective helmets. The first entry on stage is violent and harsh. It announces the return of the victorious army from the cruel war ... Wajda's Chorus is not a unified mass of people, it is the voice of public opinion, made up of the principal social forces in the world today: soldiers, technocrats, the young and the workers – the clash of the many voices, moods tones, demeanours makes very fine and intelligent theatre. *Antigone* in Wajda's interpretation is a play about the inner freedom of man, of the need to be true to oneself and to one's conscience, and of the infectious strength of good example – as regards truth, love, and sacrifice.[5]

Polityka:

It is obvious from the very onset of the play that Antigone will become the symbol of martyrdom; she aspires to this role and it is thus the Chorus see her, the Chorus in Wajda's staging being the 'hero' of the play. Wajda needs Antigone only as a counterpoint, thanks to which the Chorus can function. That is why she is so one-dimensional while the Chorus is richly varied. First it appears as the victorious 'commandos'. A moment later it becomes 'The people of Thebes', representing however that stratum of society that may be called 'The Establishment'. Dressed in modern clothes the citizens of the town pay tribute to the loathsome Creon. The next appearance of the Chorus is as youthful demonstrators. They carry banners bearing portraits of Antigone and chant the words 'Free and unsubdued!' Finally the Chorus enter dressed in grey quilted jackets and protective helmets. This time the Chorus is calm and thoughtful. It is aware of the part it must play as it speaks these lines: 'Wisdom – the only source of happiness'. And it is with this comment that Wajda's *Antigone* ends.[6]

The critic of the government-sponsored *Polityka* spitefully entitled his review 'ANTIGONE OF THE TORN POSTER', whereas the critic of the Catholic paper gave his review the following title: 'ANDRZEJ WAJDA'S GREAT MASTERPIECE'. Both critics also differed in their judgement of performances. According to *Tygodnik Powszechny*,

The title role was played by Ewa Kolasinska with great dramatic expression. Her Antigone is classic and contemporary, statuesque and tragic. Above all she is brave and convinced that the 'path' she has chosen is the right one. She knows she must die in the cause of righteousness but this decision brings her no relief. It only heightens her solitude. In her conversation with Creon her helplessness is revealed as truth: 'I came to love my fellow man and not to hate.' Kolasinska's performance is one of intensity and tragic power.[7]

By contrast, in the review of *Polityka*,

Kolasinska plays Antigone in the spirit of hatred and intolerance, on a shrill note throughout. At one point Antigone hisses: 'I came to love my fellow man and not to hate', at the same time looking as if she could kill Creon with a glance. I have never yet seen such a monstrous misrepresentation in the theatre, for the words blatantly contradict the interpretation of the character by the performer.[8]

Similar differences of opinion surrounded Tadeusz Huk's performance as Creon. Evidently, given the right combination of dramatic subject, theatrical approach, and external events any two spectators holding opposing political views will see entirely different things, though watching the same performance; hear the same words and give them contradictory meaning.
Polityka:

The use of a journalistic rationalization showing the necessity of opposing unjustified tyranny, does not excuse a slapdash artistic presentation, the mixing up of different dramatic conventions, or the imprecise and rushed interpretation.[9]

Tygodnik Powszechny:

Antigone in Wajda's interpretation can be read as a terrifying account of the crimes of tyranny, which destroys and crushes everything that stands in its way or opposes it. I however regard it as an ecstatic hymn in honour of the inner sovereignty of man.

(The remainder of the review was suppressed by the censor.)[10]

These two views of the play have not been quoted so extensively merely to show the political conditioning of theatrical criticism in Poland. Such reactions show that Wajda's *Antigone* forced the audience into a passionate response, and left no one indifferent. At the same time they indicate that the production was appreciated not so much on aesthetic or artistic grounds, but on intellectual and ideological ones. A spectator first had to declare himself for or against the ideology of the production, only afterwards perhaps perceiving what artistic means were used to convey this message. This explains why the variety and deliberate confusion of theatrical conventions deployed by Wajda here provoked one critic to see a wealth of formal devices and the other incoherent ambiguity. The use of the Chorus in several guises was given a deep, comprehensible, symbolic significance by one critic, yet the other saw it as a mere gimmick that exposed a superficial approach to Sophocles' text. Antigone herself was seen on the one hand as a fiery symbol of the inner sovereignty of man, expressed by simple and noble acting, and on the other hand as a one-dimensional and featureless character compared to the classical original, rendered with bland monotony. One supported Antigone and her protest, reflecting the underlying ideology of the production; the other sided with Creon and rejected her position, acknowledging its political force in the determination to resist it. The two-thousand-year-old controversy was resurrected to engage our thoughts and fire our emotions anew.

The truth, in the artistic if not the political sense, lay somewhere in between. Wajda's presentation of the play's moral issues in a contemporary light was, on the whole, readable although certain details were not understood by all. For instance, the reason for the use of Middle Eastern costumes for the women — a survival of the original concept — may not have been entirely clear. Alternatively, representing the Chorus as shipyard workers, with the obvious contemporary reference to the birthplace of Solidarity, could be seen as over-explicit. In short the production was sketchy and the novel interpretation bordered on intellectual simplification. But this was the price the director had to pay to obtain the confrontation with the audience that he desired.

When presenting the Chorus in familiar uniform or in the protective hard-hats of Gdansk Shipyard workers, Creon in a smart suit, and Antigone and

Ismene as Lebanese women, Wajda's purpose was not stylistic novelty or a challenge to classical ideas. He intended to penetrate a two-thousand-year-old tradition and bring the essential conflict of the Greek tragedy to life in a modern context. Indeed the production brought out the moral importance of protest precisely because — as in Sophocles' play — its protest was irrational and doomed to failure. By creating opposition to its statement the performance revealed the extent to which Creon's political pragmatism, invoking a legality that he himself has laid down, has its adherents today, especially in the East, although representatives can also be found in Western democracies. Instead of showing Creon as a tragic figure — a common practice which provides emotional justification for such an attitude — Wajda scaled down the man and diminished his justification. He intensified the fear underlying his arrogance, and the inevitability of the punishment which follows. This feature of the Cracow production of *Antigone* is pure political theatre: it not only depicts life, but also passes judgement.

In 1985, four years after martial law was declared in Poland, Ernest Bryll, a well-known Polish poet and playwright, wrote a religious dramatic poem entitled *Easter Vigil*. His suggestion that it be staged at the Teatr Ateneum in Warsaw was turned down by the censor, because of its political insinuations. Previously one of the 'official' Polish writers representing literary conformism and lauded by critics and government, now in the eyes of the authorities he was *persona non grata* as the result of a public change of heart during the Solidarity period.

Following this decision, which aroused considerable controversy, an independent production was sponsored by the Catholic Church under the artistic direction of Andrzej Wajda. To put this in its proper perspective it is necessary to realize that *every* theatre in Poland is supervised by the government and *every* public performance must by approved by the censor. When Wajda and his actors decided to bypass all the regulations governing the theatre, they were able to take advantage of a ruling that performances of a religious character, when staged on Church territory, could take place without the censor's authorization. In recent years the Church had supported many independent cultural projects, and now, for the first time, theatre was included in the 'unofficial culture' which until that time had been confined to literary readings. However familiar Polish society might be with 'illegal' literature, it was nevertheless an unprecedented and sensational event when *Easter Vigil* was staged in the Church of the *Milosierdzia Bozego* (the Lord's Mercy) in Warsaw.

40 *Easter Vigil*, Warsaw 1985. View of the audience in the Church of the Lord's Mercy in Warsaw.

Every evening hundreds of people queued for seats; the play was performed twelve times and seen by about six thousand people. A further six thousand put their names down on a 'waiting list' hoping that the play might run again. It should be noted that there had been no publicity or advertising for this play, not even any posters. Every one of these people had heard about the production by word of mouth. Their very presence at *Easter Vigil* and the ovations they gave the actors were something more than just an ordinary visit to the theatre: they were a manifestation of support for independent culture and therefore, to a large extent, a political manifestation.[11]

Wajda's decision to produce a play that had been banned by the authorities was not merely a gesture challenging the Polish cultural Establishment. It was also his return to explicitly political theatre, even though again in this case the play was political in metaphor and symbolism rather than in its formal aspect. Rather than any resemblance to modern *agit-prop*, Bryll's *Easter Vigil* was based on the religious tradition of the Passion Plays and in accordance with this tradition the play was first performed on Good Friday.

Its story is taken from the Gospel, the main character being the Apostle known as 'doubting Thomas', and is set in the room where the Apostles had eaten the Last Supper with Christ. Now they are in hiding after the Crucifixion. In the ensuing action, the crushed and frightened hunted men try to analyze their situation; they endeavour to comprehend why the Cause, until recently so near victory, has been totally defeated. Naturally, they begin to look for blame amongst themselves with bitter remonstrations, speculating on the subject of betrayal, provocation, etc. . . . They are visited in their hiding-place by sympathizers of the movement; one brings news of Judas' suicide, another a proposal from their persecutors to reach an agreement on the basis of political compromise. Finally, Mary Magdalene brings the news of the Resurrection. This is the catalyst for the main dramatic focus of the play: the intellectual conflict between the zealous believers awaiting their Lord, and doubting Thomas. Finally Thomas leaves to search for Christ, returning with no news, only to learn that Jesus had appeared to the others in his absence. The play ends with a symbolic vision of Christ and the words of Thomas: 'Yes, I see him and recognize him but I must touch him.'

On the surface there seems little reason for such a poetic, overtly religious play to trigger sufficiently intense feelings in Poland in 1985 that the authorities should have suppressed it while the people greeted it with great enthusiasm. However, what both censor and audience understood is that a deeper, metaphorical meaning, with a direct bearing on the situation in their own country, lurked beneath this Gospel story. *Easter Vigil* analyzed the situation after the shattering of an ideal, which up to that point had seemed impermeable, unchallengeable. The transposition of ideology for religious belief was easy for Poles who had been taught that Communism was the Party of the working classes, and were now being given daily demonstrations of the system betraying its official principles. Even stronger feelings, however, were triggered by the perfectly readable reference to the most recent historical events: the triumphant rise and sudden fall of the Solidarity Movement. As a result there was a strong identification with the Apostles as they agonized over reasons for the failure of faith. Finally, the Resurrection was a heartening symbol of hope and faith in the ultimate restoration of true values, and Wajda's staging emphasized the topical issues of the drama without losing its religious characteristics. The play was performed – extremely appropriately – in a ruined church which was in process of being restored, and the bare brick wall gave the effect of the early Christian meeting-place.

The staging of the opening scene of the Last Supper was reminiscent of Leonardo da Vinci's famous painting. After this prologue the action took place in the aisle with the main doors as a background. Each time these doors were opened for entries or exits the lights from neighbouring houses in the street were visible, and the screech of police sirens could be heard from outside: an immediate reminder of martial law, when police sirens were heard constantly in Poland. At the same time, it directly enhanced the tense atmosphere of the dramatic situation. Since their performance verged on illegality, the gap between the actors and their characterization was minimal. To emphasize this they were dressed in modern-day clothes and one of the characters – the mysterious Stranger – arrived in a car which he would park outside the main entrance, leaving the motor running. He has come to persuade Mary Magdalene to flee the country with him. Not unsurprisingly, it was this updating of the religious drama that met with most criticism from the official press.

Easter Vigil was not a play that inspired directorial fireworks. The production was very simple, theatrically speaking, but its impact on the social and political awareness of the Polish audience was considerable. The casting of popular actors was also effective, indicating that the feelings of ordinary people were shared by well-known personalities. For instance, Krystyna Janda, the actress who had portrayed the heroine in both *Man of Marble* and *Man of Iron*, played Mary Magdalene. But, above all, the play itself manifested the political views of a group of Polish artists during a particularly tense time. Its performance was political theatre which made its point in the calm reflective tone of religion, rather than by shock tactics.

8 Summing up: the theatre of Andrzej Wajda

The study of Wajda's theatrical work from *A Hatful of Rain* in 1959 to *Crime and Punishment* in 1984 or *Easter Vigil* in 1985 does not embrace the whole of his dramatic output during this period. His productions outside Poland and their reception have yet to be discussed; and it is appropriate to separate these from the mainstream of his creative work in the theatre because the most essential and significant aspect of that work is its intimate connection with Polish society and Polish culture. Though his approach and technical achievements, his handling of the dramatic texts and working methods with actors may serve as general models, his achievements are also a demonstration that the vital element of theatre is the immediacy and directness of its contact with a specific audience. To gain international stature it must have strong local roots, and the philosophical and psychological base of Wajda's productions lies in their national specificity, something which I hope has been repeatedly made clear in this book.

Overseas Wajda's theatre has taken varied forms: some productions have been seen at International Theatre Festivals, others have transferred to foreign stages. Polish theatre companies and especially the Stary Teatr troupe have been invited to perform abroad, and occasionally Wajda himself has produced a play outside Poland. To this we may add his film adaptations of plays such as *The Wedding* and *Danton* that have been distributed worldwide. *Play Strindberg* was the first production abroad to draw attention to the fact that Andrzej Wajda is not only a film-maker but also a brilliant theatre director. However it was not until the double triumph of *The Possessed* at the World Theatre Season in London in 1972 and 1973, that his stage work became well known internationally. Sir Peter Daubeny, its artistic director at the time, who had seen *The Possessed* earlier in Cracow, wrote: 'This wonderful production made an extremely strong impression upon me. I immediately signed a contract with the Stary Teatr to bring it to London for the World Theatre Season. The play was an enormous success with the public as well as the critics. It was the culminating point of the Festival.'[1] In this connection it is relevant to quote Robert Brustein's 1973 evaluation in the *Observer*:

At the very first moment of contact with this wonderful Polish Company one sensed the overpowering exaltation that the audience felt during the Moscow Art Theatre's productions in its prime. In spite of the fact that Wajda's *Possessed* was already performed in London last year, I see no sign of this production's influence on British actors, or

Summing up

directors, nor on their approach to contemporary theatre. I find this amazing! One could have expected that such an evening would radically change our views on the priorities of today's theatre. In short this production is a milestone confirming, in one fell swoop, the supremacy of theatre over the other arts, as a vehicle of active philosophy and a force of instantaneous emotional reaction.[2]

The Possessed was also seen in other European countries but it was the second Dostoyevsky adaptation, *Nastasya Filippovna*, that made the greater international impact. The improvisation based on *The Idiot* became the 'hallmark' of Polish theatre on a level with Grotowski's 'Laboratorium' and Tomaszewski's mime theatre 'Pantomima'. The Stary Teatr presented *Nastasya Filippovna* at festivals in Edinburgh, Nancy, Caracas, Buenos Aires, West Berlin, Karlsruhe, Dubrovnik, Florence, Madrid, Stockholm, Amsterdam, Helsinki, Budapest, Rome, Turin and Milan as well as other German and Italian cities. Soon after opening in Poland, *Crime and Punishment* was already being performed in Spain and West Germany, and many other international invitations have followed.[3] Owing to the universality of their themes, Wajda's productions based on Dostoyevsky's works have become his best-known theatrical achievements abroad.

In 1972 Wajda was invited to Moscow to direct David Rabe's play *Sticks and Bones* at the renowned Sovremiennik Theatre. The main part was played by the famous Russian actor Oleg Tabakow. The play was a success and, as the director said himself, brought him valuable contact with Russian actors and with a theatre where dedication to Art came first and foremost.

Wajda's subsequent experience abroad was less fortunate. Invited in 1972 to direct Dürrenmatt's new play *Der Mitmacher (The Partner)* in the Schauspielhaus in Zurich, he accepted, and rehearsals began. Almost immediately, however, a sharp conflict arose between Wajda and the author, who interfered and tried to impose his own concept. As a result Wajda withdrew from the production and had his name removed from the poster. Undeterred, Dürrenmatt completed rehearsals himself and produced a total disaster. Though he defended Dürrenmatt the writer against Dürrenmatt the director in an open letter published in the Swiss press, Wajda's only comment on these events was as follows: 'In my ignorance I thought that Dürrenmatt would permit me to direct his play, that this was the reason he had summoned me, confident that I could achieve something on the basis of his work. But he turned out to be narrow-minded, which is sometimes the case with men of genius. We cannot blame them for that. I only blame myself that I became involved in the whole affair.'[4] This incident, which occurred relatively early in Wajda's theatrical career, seemed to confirm that he flourished best on home ground.

In 1974 Robert Brustein, who had been so enthusiastic about the London performance of *The Possessed*, became artistic director of the Yale Repertory Theatre. He invited Wajda to stage his production of the play again, this time with young American actors. Amongst the students of the Yale School of Drama was Meryl Streep who played Liza Drozdow. Elzbieta Czyzewska, an outstanding Polish actress who had settled in the United States, played Maria Lebiadkin. However, although Wajda literally transposed the play in its entirety from the Cracow stage, there was a crucial difference between the Polish and American productions. This came from the acting and was, in fact, unintended by Wajda. The Polish actors had been experienced professionals, one could say the best in the land, whereas the Americans were inexperienced youngsters or in some cases still drama students. In addition, their understanding of Dostoyevsky was inevitably less complete than that of Poles with their close links to the Russian mentality and culture. As a consequence the Yale production lacked the dramatic intensity of its Cracow forerunner – the existential aspect of Dostoyevsky was emphasized, the Slavonic, violent and emotional, played down. However it was much acclaimed and Wajda returned in 1977 to direct the equally popular *White Wedding* by Tadeusz Rozewicz, which touched on topical issues of the social and sexual emancipations of women.

The play – a sexual comedy – tells of the sexual initiation of two sisters 'from a good home' at the turn of the century, when sex was still very much a taboo subject. One of the sisters becomes virtually obsessed with the idea of the 'forbidden fruit'. However, the struggle with the 'sexual demon' is portrayed in a light-hearted and tongue-in-cheek manner. Although the play seemed a far cry from Wajda's normal interests, he wanted to try his hand at straight comedy which for him was still as yet almost uncharted territory. Moreover in the seventies the *belle époque* was very much in fashion, and erotic subjects were being portrayed on stage in an increasingly daring way. Krystyna Zachwatowicz designed pastel, sickly sweet costumes and sets, emphasizing the playful conventions of the production, while Wajda imposed a stylized and highly exaggerated form of acting on his young actors. In effect, Wajda had produced the play very much in the style of a dramatist like Witkacy (incidentally, his first choice had been to produce a Witkacy play), with demonic sexual obsessions being largely superseded by an absurdly grotesque light-comedy style. So it was perhaps logical that Wajda chose to direct *They* by Witkacy, the only work by this author he ever produced, when invited to the Centre Dramatique at Nanterre in France in 1979. It appeared under the French title *Ils ont déjà occupé la ville voisine* in 1980.

Stanislaw Ignacy Witkacy's plays of the 1920s and 1930s proclaimed the end of European civilization, and he committed suicide on the first day of the

Second World War as if to confirm his own convictions. *They* is his most prophetic work. The main character, Balandaszek, is an aesthete, art-lover and self-taught philosopher. He and his mistress Spika conduct never-ending philosophical discussions, believing in the enduring dominance of intellectual order and the liberating nature of Art. However, their refined world is under threat: 'They' are coming – the barbarians who intend to abolish art and replace all existing philosophies with their own – an uncanny forecast of what was to happen in Europe under Nazi totalitarianism. *They*, like all of Witkacy's plays, is presented in the style of the absurd and grotesque, where philosophical truths are articulated by farcical satire and caricature.

In his version of the play at Nanterre Wajda decided on a bold interpretation. 'They' were women who had taken over the world and were subjecting it ruthlessly to hard-line feminist principles, and consistent with this textual revision he cast Spika as a man. The part was played by Andrzej Seweryn, an actor he had often used before and who now lives permanently in France, while Wojciech Pszoniak was imported for Balandaszek. All Wajda had intended, faithful to the satiric absurdity of Witkacy's drama, was to poke lighthearted fun at the rapidly expanding feminist movement by portraying women as the mirror-image of the authoritarian men they displace. However, the critics and the feminists themselves treated this 'joke' with deadly seriousness. Wajda was accused of being a chauvinist, a misogynist and even a reactionary. The further cultural implications of the 'battle of the sexes' were overlooked, as was the humour. Wajda says today that obviously his production had been 'too progressive' for France, where in order not to be considered conservative, one had to pander to the feminist movement.

Even from such a brief summary, it is clear that Wajda took up a wide variety of experimental challenges in his work outside Poland, sometimes of a very different nature from his usual interests at home. In spite of their generally recognized high standard, however, none of these foreign productions attained the exuberance, richness and power of vision which characterize his greatest achievements in Poland.

What then is 'the theatre of Andrzej Wajda'? What underlying thread binds his individual works into an artistic and intellectual whole? The answer is not easy to find, especially since Wajda, unlike many of his contemporaries, has not formulated a philosophy, nor based his works on any particular theory. He has often talked about theatre, and many of his comments are quoted here, but these are usually practical remarks on particular productions, or else expressions of personal feelings and general outlook. They are not however, strictly speaking, theoretical and they do not present a single attitude to theatre. It could even be said that Wajda deliberately avoids restricting

41   Andrzej Wajda (right) and Maciej Karpinski during rehearsals of *The Danton Affair*, Sofia (Bulgaria) 1978.

himself to a single doctrine, moving freely among the theatre's traditions and combining conventions as diverse as the theatre of Wyspianski and the Japanese *Bunraku* theatre.

Despite this variety and nonconformity, Andrzej Wajda remains faithful to general principles that – in various ways – link such diverse works as *November Night* and *The Emigrants*, *The Possessed* and *Antigone*. These principles derive from a characteristically Polish theatrical tradition, which entails a strong sense of moral responsibility towards the Polish nation and invariably leads Polish artists to favour certain subjects and a specific theatrical form. This tradition takes its origin from the Romantic Movement. The greatest Polish writers of that movement, Mickiewicz, Slowacki and Krasinski; were all political exiles. They all chose nationalistic patriotic themes, and the classic plays of this period such as *Forefathers' Eve* by Mickiewicz, *The Undivine Comedy* by Krasinski or *Kordian* by Slowacki remain to this day the deepest

Summing up

analysis of Polish national consciousness. However, the realization that their works were unlikely to be performed meant that these writers had no need to comply with the restrictive conventions, and their form is so loose they could well be contemporary plays. As a result they created a style of theatre, at least on paper, that was only put into practice after the major theatrical reforms of the twentieth century. And Wyspianski, who initiated modern theatre in Poland, was literally their 'heir': his reforming activities began with the staging of *Forefathers' Eve* and *Kordian*, bridging the gap between Romanticism and contemporary Polish theatre.

Wyspianski also formulated a programme for a 'vast theatre', monumental and poetic, which combined the development and expansion of Romantic theatre concepts with the theories of the early twentieth-century reformers. Wyspianski — poetically — expressed his programme as follows:

> I see my theatre as vast,
> With huge, airy spaces
> Thronging with people and shadows;
> Their drama gives me awareness.[5]

This 'vast theatre' can accommodate people and ghosts; it freely uses the monumental form, mirroring the most vital conflicts of the past and present. It is also a 'theatre of painting', where the 'huge open spaces' are filled by a lofty artistic vision, and its correspondence to Edward Gordon Craig's theories led him to name Wyspianski as one of the most outstanding theatrical reformers in twentieth-century Europe in his preface to *The Art of Theatre* (1905).

The tradition of Wyspianski's 'vast theatre' is still alive in Poland today, and every artist grapples with it in his own way, radical theorists such as Kantor and Grotowski not excluded. The essence of the avant-garde and progressive movements in Poland is an ability to establish a vivid dialogue with the past and to contribute creatively to the age-old cycle of change and transformation. Romanticism is not treated as a historical relic or dead language but as the living, creative spirit of art: the internal tension, the conflict which is the origin of real drama. Romanticism, understood in this way, has been perhaps most exactly defined by Ludwik Flaszen, Grotowski's long-time collaborator at the Teatr Laboratorium:

Romanticism is reborn again and again, not resurrected as a corpse with a painted face. It reappears in Wajda's explosive, sensual visions, Swinarski's demonic sense of humour, or in the 'complete act' of Grotowski, who, whilst continuing the Romantic tradition, rejected the grand staging of the 'vast theatre'. Romantic theatre is not just the celebration of a rite to confirm an established truth, but a challenge that forcibly undermines the certainty of our world view. It is neither verse dialogue or poetic prose, nor the expression of vivid pictures [which are commonly associated with it], but dissonant, sharp contradictions and tense conflicts. Not a passive, pious, respect for values but, as it were, a blasphemous test which brings to light their paradoxical similarities and intriguing associations. It must not attempt to reach us merely intellectually, wrapped in Pathos and a poetic mist; it must shake us to the very core. It must not only express truth, and convince us of it, but hurl us into a complex process where, by trial and error, we find our own truth. I would say the true Romantic performance is an initiation by shock.[6]

Paradoxically, Andrzej Wajda has never directed any of the great works of the Polish Romantics. Yet all his productions are examples of Romantic theatre as described by Flaszen. This is the source of their emotional impact: the nostalgic pathos of *November Night* or the spasmodic atmosphere of *The Possessed*. In this respect the evolution of Wajda's theatre is characteristic: those two plays belong to that 'vast theatre' where all the machinery of the stage is deployed in the service of unbridled imagination. Then a reduction ensued: from the simplicity of *The Danton Affair* to the basic asceticism of *Nastasya Filippovna* and *Crime and Punishment*. But in these very productions we see no diminution of the Romantic battle of opposing forces but rather their intensification. Even if their staging no longer corresponded to 'vast theatre', their emotional impact still represented an 'initiation by shock'. A comparable tension was evident even in his modest productions such as *The Emigrants* or *Conversations with the Executioner*, and it is this tension that creates the emotional temperature by which 'the theatre of Andrzej Wajda' is instantly recognizable. None of his mature productions were passive, giving merely aesthetic or intellectual satisfaction. Their strength consisted in multiple dimensions and controversial ambiguities. In short, the Romantic tradition is the common thread that runs through the whole of Wajda's immensely varied theatre work, and he counts as its most creative and innovatory exponent.

One of the vital elements of this heritage is a strong sense of historical and social responsibility. Theatre does not exist in a vacuum; it is a living component of a nation's vicissitudes and a live commentary on contemporary times. Hence one of the most important aspects of Wajda's mature productions is their topicality, which motivates his search for the intellectual and emotional links to classical or even ancient plays and his choice of contemporary works. Whatever their explicit subject, the bottom line in each of his productions is the question of freedom, existential as well as political. For any artist – but particularly one living in Poland where the conflicting demands of discipline and free expression or cultural norms and radical renewal are inseparable from the wider dimension of foreign domination and national aspirations – this is a basic dilemma; and each of Wajda's major works from *The Possessed* to *Crime and Punishment* exemplifies its problems. What his analysis has consistently demonstrated is that the moral law within

Summing up

a man is stronger than coercion, repression and evil, be it individual or collective, and conversely this political conclusion has personal implications. In the face of repeated opposition it has served as an artistic imperative to committed work expressing the liberty of conscience. Yet for Wajda creative freedom has never been an end in itself. 'What did I need that freedom for?', asks Wajda.

> I wanted to be free so that I could tune in to my nation's soul and express its fears, hopes and dreams... That is exactly how any artist should put his freedom to use. However, an artist must sometimes tell his nation things that it does not want to hear. In order to do that, he needs, as it were, double freedom: he must have freedom from authority and freedom from his public. Only the greatest deserve this freedom and we bow our heads in acknowledgement before them.[7]

From this standpoint the theatre is not only, or even primarily, an aesthetic manifestation. A production must also be a vehicle for a philosophical, moral and political message. As a director Wajda is not merely a bystander but an active participant in the history of his own country, and sensitive to international events, who tries to shape the world with his art. The artist with a mission is also part of the Romantic inheritance, as is the spirit that impels Wajda's continuous artistic explorations. His substantial achievements and international reputation have not turned him into a 'classic' and he remains restless and unpredictable. 'He is constantly critical', writes Stefan Morawski:

> where others are silent and hypocritical he is ever ready to awaken the conscience and unsettle official optimism. His conviction that the deepest artistic function is a critical attitude, drawing attention to negative episodes in history in the light of positive ones, makes him one of the most 'romantic' perpetrators of the Romantic tradition today. The fact that his criticism does not always please the bureaucrats may be considered normal. The function of art means something quite different to them, they need support for their current actions. It is much worse when artists and critics sacrifice their integrity to raise their hands in praise, as though they were unaware, or knowingly wished to forget, that an artist who behaves thus destroys his potential and fails in his duty: he discovers nothing and loses what little he possessed. Future researchers will, no doubt, explain more precisely why Wajda chose certain works and not others, why he was drawn to history as his main subject. However, when viewing Wajda's creative output today it is already evident that he has an exceptional ability for portraying the contemporary world through symbols and archetypes. I would have no hesitation in describing him as a visionary, who seeks in the past, the best possible road to the future.[8]

Despite his commitment to the missionary role of art and the unifying theme that underlies all his work, Wajda's approach is pragmatic. His eclecticism, the shifting variety of styles from one production to another, is designed to stimulate spectators by countering their expectations. To provoke an audience into reflection on historical matters, contemporary issues, or their own biases and beliefs, the theatre must first be exciting and vital: something that contrasts with the usual presentation of serious drama, at least in Poland. In Wajda's own words;

> there seems to be a common conviction here that plays must be performed slowly, at a distance, in darkness and silence. This is what I experience all too frequently when I enter a Polish theatre. In my opinion theatre should be loud, bright, clear and immediate. I am quite certain of that. This is my first consideration, whatever I happen to be directing. I think that any research into how the theatre affects the public in Poland would end up by forbidding such slow, dark, distant productions, for they effectively numb the audience. The audience must be aroused. The spectator must feel his blood flowing faster, in order to be stimulated into action.[9]

Finally, to evaluate any director it is necessary to examine some basic questions about working methods in the most practical, everyday sense. How does he analyze the text and direct his actors, and – in Wajda's case – how does he harmonize all the elements of theatre to create such 'orchestrated' productions?

For Andrzej Wajda, work in the theatre is not just the putting into practice of established principles. The process of creating is above all the discovery and exposition of that which is hidden, which is why he seems at first glance to favour improvisation as a working method. It conveys the impression that a production takes shape spontaneously, without previous preparation. As a director he utilizes the element of surprise: it is as if the team of actors working with him are sucked into a whirlpool of activity that can only be controlled by communal creative energy.

Wajda is not a director who arrives at rehearsals with a meticulously marked script and piles of notes. He does not proceed to block, with great precision, scenes he has previously worked out. He prefers to begin work on a project in front of his team of actors and apparently without a ready concept. His purpose is to create a desire in them to arrive at an unknown goal by team effort. If all is known in advance and laid out from beginning to end, work on a production merely becomes the laborious execution of a pre-conceived programme. To quote Wajda:

> Directing does not mean imposing every minute detail of one's own vision upon the actors, but forging them together so securely that they cannot come apart, enabling them to repeat this process at every performance. If theatre is to be a creative art, one must induce the actors, playing the same part every evening, to live through the drama anew each time. For me, it is this that proves the unique ability of a director. All the rest such as the staging, directing actors, planning the set, can be done by any professional. All those things are of no significance.[10]

At the same time it is clearly not strictly true to say that Wajda only develops the overall concept of a production through rehearsal, and in fact few of his projects are undertaken completely without previous preparation. There are

Summing up

42 Andrzej Wajda (right) with actors during a rehearsal of *Crime and Punishment*, Cracow 1984.

some subjects, some works which dog an artist for years before he finally realizes them. During this time they are thought through, elaborated, even fixed in their essentials. It is later, when putting these ideas into practice, that Wajda gives the impression of entirely spontaneous work in order to provoke others into making the same creative effort. In any event, regardless of the duration and character of the preparations, before work commences at least two things must be established in advance, as a foundation on which the production is built. These two elements are: the general outline of the set, and the casting of the main parts.

For instance at the start of rehearsals for *The Danton Affair*, it had already been decided that the action would take place in the centre, amongst the audience. Similarly in *The Emigrants* the idea of the bright lights and screen was adopted from the start, while Wajda himself says that he could not conceive staging a play without a clear picture of the set in his mind even though the actual design may undergo many changes during the preparation period. Its details take shape alongside all the other elements, and Wajda has given an example of how this works in practice:

There were no drawn plans as such for the design of *November Night* or *The Possessed*. I simply decided on the background of clouds, then sent the designer to a museum to get the idea from paintings.[11] I had the mud made up. I wanted real mud but that was impossible as the play was being performed in repertory, so we made the mud as near the real thing as possible. I choose the furniture and had screens constructed; but no sketches were ever made as it was not necessary. Everything evolved on stage, according to the needs of the action, lighting etc.[12]

To illustrate one need only compare the existing sketch of the setting for *The Emigrants* with what was actually constructed on stage: when the set was finally put up it comprised all the same components but arranged quite differently. Even then changes were introduced almost up to the last minute. The back wall of *The Emigrants'* cubby hole was designed out of material imitating a cellar wall. Wajda ordered part of it to be removed and wire meshing to be put in its place, even though the decision had far-reaching consequences not only for the visual quality of the play but also for the blocking. In his normal practice, however, it is the particular requirements of the staging that determine the final composition, every detail of which is personally supervised. When it is necessary to choose furniture or a bigger prop, Wajda will go to the storeroom himself. For him, the choice of a table or an armchair, or the book that should be lying on that table, is also a creative element.

The casting is of equal importance to Wajda. Even if his political stance and his desire for the widest possible audience has prevented the establishment of his own company, he relies on actors who are known to him, seeing them in definite parts that are suitable for them personally and that exploit their artistic capacities to the fullest. By contrast to his film work, where Wajda prefers to avoid known faces and to discover and form new talent, in the theatre he expects a creative partnership from his actors. Thus Wajda has no common language with any actors who treat their profession merely as a job or those without personality. An actor who substitutes technique for thought quickly loses his confidence and becomes relegated to the margins of his productions. However he has considerable time and patience for those fired by an inner flame, who do not seek an easy way out, actors who show initiative and struggle to find their character. He allows them to falter and make mistakes, but he expects them to be emotionally committed to their profession. The actors of the Stary Teatr, however different their personalities – the passionate Pszoniak, the intellectual Stuhr, the seeming cynic and eternal adversary Nowicki, and the analytical Radziwilowicz – these are the director's partners.

Unless perhaps in a large ensemble scene, Wajda rarely orders the actors about or positions them on stage. As a director he expects the situation to evolve naturally, dictated by the actor's emotion. He indicates only where a scene is to begin, the 'climate' and the atmosphere. For Wajda the composition of a scene or the actors' moves are merely a framework, a background which takes shape only when the characters find their psychological truth. Directing is creating a situation which provokes such a truth, and this premise is reinforced by his belief that theatre, and therefore each theatrical role, must be live, created as it were on the spot, before the very eyes of the audience. It is a transitory moment, and the most a director can do is create favourable working conditions; the rest belongs to the actor.

Wajda's basic advice to the actor is summed up in the following maxims:

> Act – don't talk!
> Attack – don't reminisce!
> Move from the word to the action.
> This is a fight: strike a blow, then defend yourself, retreat, attack.
> Be aware of the other players constantly.
> With whom are you interacting?
> Who are your opponents?
> Remember that acting is not what happened yesterday but what is happening now, in the present tense.[13]

Wajda's stress is on the importance of immediacy (the present tense), intensity (this is a fight) and interaction, not only between the players (with whom you are interacting) but also with the world at large (who are the opponents). This last element especially echoes the Romantic concept of theatre as an art form with a mission, and when these three 'requirements' are met the acting in Wajda's productions bears the characteristic traits of emotional tension and psychological truth.

While I have drawn attention to the creative aspect of the choices made by Wajda, beginning with casting, through to the most detailed elements of the production – and I consider the skill in making such choices a vital component of director's technique – an equally important aspect is Wajda's ability to provoke a specific creative atmosphere during rehearsals, which involves all who are taking part in it, regardless of their function. Trusting his actors and giving them the freedom to create, he is able to abandon his own preconceptions and has demonstrated his openness to other points of view, which alone can form the basis of the teamwork required for putting on a play. However, by itself this 'negative capability' would be insufficient. It has to be accompanied by another, undefinable quality, the ability to inspire a company to work in a united spirit, towards common goals, and Wajda's function as 'inspirator' rather than traditional director can be best seen in *Nastasya Filippovna* (see pp. 75–9 above).

It would be appropriate here to examine how Wajda works on the text. He is one of those people who, whatever they read, always read their 'own book'. Indeed, with certain types of material Wajda apparently does not read what is printed in the text at all – the letters, words and sentences – but reads 'in images', his own images divining the sense or encompassing the feeling and atmosphere of each scene. The results of such an unliterary approach are paradoxical: however superficial in a critical sense, it is capable of offering profound insights into the essence of a work. In short, as a director his approach to a literary text always focusses on the simple question: 'What is this about?' After finding the most basic, human meaning of a given fragment, he then searches for a method of communicating this insight in its fundamental form to his audience. During rehearsals he also questions his actors to establish the meaning of a given gesture, intonation, move, or emotional state. Only once all these questions have beeen satisfactorily answered does he consider how to shape the whole scene in practical terms, putting it together and scaling it down to form a unity. The appropriateness of Wajda's dramaturgical resolutions, which flow from marrying the interpretation of the text with his own subjective response, is thus rarely due to intellectual analysis. The staging is never derived from the kind of detailed background research into a period of social history or a writer's biography that characterizes the work of a director like Peter Stein. Rather its adequacy in expressing the theme depends on the inner meaning of a text resonating in the director's consciousness. Yet at the same time Wajda's theatre – picturesque, visionary, emotional – is in fact a theatre that feeds off literature. As he himself has declared: 'Theatre in our European tradition derives from the word, from literature, the Greeks, Shakespeare, Chekhov. This is its source while the beautiful ephemera of the artists, the designers and the producers is a small part of the process, created only to awaken and stimulate the true theatre of words.'[14] This sounds like an outright defence of pure literature in the theatre, and it is all the more significant for having been spoken by a director who is himself a designer and a visual artist.

A more accurate way of putting it would be that Wajda treats the text he is working on as a 'partner'. While rehearsing *Nastasya Filippovna* he frequently referred to Dostoyevsky's novel, keeping a check on his own ideas as he went along. But the intention was by no means to present *The Idiot* line by line. On the contrary, the guiding concept was that great literature, through its profundity, achieved by detailed descriptions of human behaviour and shrewd analysis of character, should become a stimulant for the actors, who in turn had to create equally detailed stage characters. Wajda's premise seems to be that the lives of real people, literary characters, and stage figures are three entirely different things. In order to shape the latter successfully it is necessary to know as much as possible about the other two; but at the same time it is essential to avoid being excessively influenced, or even limited, by that knowledge. The point is not to imitate life or illustrate literature, but to find methods — within the theatre's potential — to transfer the other two kinds of 'life' onto the stage. At first it might appear that the dramatic material is being unceremoniously divorced from its origin by deviating from the original course of events and characters, and that if the exact words of the text are not religiously respected the author's ideas are being perverted. Yet the most important thing for Wajda is whether a given production, whatever the methods employed, accurately conveys the author's original vision to the spectator. He sees his role always as speaking for the author — whether Dürrenmatt or Dostoyevsky — rather than for himself. It is clearly paradoxical, however, to speak of loyalty to the author as far as Wajda is concerned. There are few directors with such a personal, distinctive and original voice.

Precision in the development of thought is undoubtedly one of the salient features of Wajda's theatre. The words used by Wittgenstein in the preface to *Tractatus Logico-Philosophicus* could be Andrzej Wajda's motto: 'Anything that can be said, can be said clearly, but that which cannot be spoken of should not be mentioned.'

Epilogue

On the 21 June 1986 Wajda's production of *The Vengeance*, a comedy by Alexander Fredro (1793–1876), was premiered in Cracow. *The Vengeance* may be a brilliant masterpiece, yet as a Polish critic, Boy-Zelenski, commented in his book *Settling Accounts with Fredro*:

> It is a fact which cannot be disputed that Fredro is one of the world's greatest writers of comedy, one of the small number of born comic geniuses. On the other hand, it is also a fact that he is these things only for us, that his contribution to world drama has been virtually nil. This in no way depreciates his value. In this respect he merely shares the fate of all our best writers.[1]

Unfortunately this appraisal is only too correct as far as Polish culture is concerned. It could be extended to cover not only Fredro, but also Wyspianski, Witkacy and even Slowacki or Mickiewicz. It is Wajda's awareness of this that led him to select little-known plays by Rozewicz or Witkacy for production abroad once his reputation had been firmly established by his Dostoyevsky trilogy; and in this, his most recent work, the almost invisible, neutral quality of his direction could be seen as a further attempt to broaden the appreciation of Polish culture through his art. Indeed the fact that *The Vengeance* is among the most inaccessible of Polish dramas may have been a factor in its selection by Wajda. The style of the play, with its complex plot, verse dialogue and reliance on verbal wit, makes it resistant to translation.[2]

The play, which gives a colourful picture of the old-time gentry in Poland and is based on the Romeo and Juliet motif, is a standard piece in the repertoire of Polish theatre. Since it has already been staged in every possible style and context, the average director is now reduced to searching for hidden meanings in the text in order to produce a novel interpretation that would justify its restaging. As Wajda commented:

> In order to stage *The Vengeance* in the Polish theatre we seem to need a special anniversary, a national disaster or some other important event ... So we always have to watch *The Vengeance* on stage in some special context: social, political or national and we cannot simply enjoy this gift from heaven ... For me, *The Vengeance* is a wonderful straightforward, theatrical masterpiece and in this sense a heavenly gift. I, for one, would like to see it produced and performed in this spirit.[3]

And this was precisely the spirit of Wajda's production: a straightforward rendering of the play, just as Fredro wrote it. The staging is simple, the

43   *The Vengeance*, Cracow 1986. The Notary (Jerzy Trela) and fearful Papkin (Jerzy Radziwilowicz).

production modest, yet full of the fun that emanates from pure, live theatre. It is as if the director were drawing breath after the tension and gravity of his later work. At the same time it is a manifestation of his faith in the ability of theatre to move and thrill us even in the hardest of times. This faith is passed on to his actors, and so we see Jerzy Radziwilowicz – the actor who portrayed Myshkin in the heavy drama of *Nastasya Filippovna*, and the hero of the harrowing political films *Man of Marble* and *Man of Iron* – happily portraying a comical, boastful coward and trickster. (He played the part alternately with Jerzy Stuhr.)

This does not mean that Wajda and his actors have abandoned their artistic principles. The production is a reminder that the indispensable function of

44 *The Vengeance*, Cracow 1986. Papkin (Jerzy Stuhr, centre) tells his incredible story to the Cup-bearer (Jerzy Binczycki, left) and the Steward.

theatre is to entertain — without which any serious purpose becomes lost — that a director's achievement cannot be separated from the experience of live performance and that its essence always escapes critical analysis. Even a study such as this, by someone who has collaborated closely with the director over many years, can do little more than record externals, and the last word should be left to Andrzej Wajda himself. A Wajda exhibition was mounted in Cracow to coincide with the premiere of *The Vengeance* at the Stary Teatr (and also with the director's sixtieth birthday), and Wajda wrote in the catalogue:

What exactly is directing in the theatre? Who is the director? At the time theatre came into being there was no role for a director as such, and for centuries afterwards his job was not clearly defined. What then is the hallmark of his activity? . . . I am asking myself this and many other questions at the time of the exhibitions's opening . . . Amassed here are notes,

Epilogue

drawings, photographs and documents. These things can give a clue to my work in the theatre, my struggle with concept, direction and also the technical side of the production. However they only manage to form a vague image of the actual task at hand; much in the same way that a map of a battle, however carefully drawn, cannot convey the blood, sweat and tears of the real combat . . .

Some years ago in Paris, I saw a startling exhibition by a conceptual artist. He had segregated and placed in a glass showcase various items that had belonged to an old woman: numerous saucepans, mats, reels of cotton, cushions, shoes, all neatly stacked and numbered, which was supposed to prove that this old lady really existed. As I viewed this presentation I wanted to cry out in horror: surely this poor woman was once loved by someone, perhaps even adored. She must have loved too, she may have lived for someone . . . Such things do not bear testimony to what is most important.

And as I stand here at this exhibition, something inside me cries: Listen to me. I have been loved and admired. In London the standing ovation after the first night of *The Possessed* lasted twenty minutes. During *Nastasya Filippovna* in Buenos Aires the candles and oil lamps went out from lack of air and the audience remained entranced . . . but my cry dwindles and dies out, for on the exhibition walls I am confronted by merely inanimate objects bearing no trace of the pulsating exuberance of the actual theatrical productions. For theatre by its very nature is transitory, it moves and amuses only those participating here and now.

Notes

1. Introduction

1. A. Wajda: 'In Theatre . . .', *Teatr*, 1974, no. 14.
2. The interview for *Trybuna Ludu*, 1976, no. 107.
3. Stefan Morawski: 'The Main Topic of Andrzej Wajda', *Dialog*, 1975, no. 9.
4. Wajda was able to return to film-making in Poland in 1985 when he made *The Chronicle of Love Accidents*.
5. Transcript of the interview granted to West Deutsche Rundfunk, October 1984 (excerpts).

2. Stylistic experimentation

1. For example, Konrad Eberhardt in the magazine *Film*, 1960, no. 36.
2. *Gazeta Krakowska*, 25 July 1959.
3. 'In Theatre . . .' It should be noted here that when Zbigniew Cybulski was killed under the wheels of a train some years later, Wajda made his film *Everything for Sale*, depicting the fascinating, unique personality of the actor.
4. J.P. Gawlik in *Zycie Literackie*, 1959, no. 28.
5. Leon Schiller: 'The New Theatre in Poland: Stanislaw Wyspianski', in *The Mask*, 1909, nos. 1–3 and 4–6.
6. *The Tragical History of Hamlet, Prince of Denmark Freshly Re-Read and Re-Thought by Stanislaw Wyspianski*, Cracow, 1905.
7. *Film*, 1960, no. 36.
8. A. Wajda: 'In Theatre . . .'
9. Andrzej Wroblewski in the magazine *Teatr*, 1960, no. 21.
10. *Il Messagero*, 22 September 1982.
11. A. Wajda: 'In Theatre . . .'
12. *Trybuna Ludu*, 1961, no. 11.
13. *Sztandar Mlodych*, 1963, no. 64.
14. *Kurier Polski*, 17 March 1963.
15. A. Wajda: 'In Theatre . . .'
16. Bogdan Wojdowski: *Proba bez kostiumu* [Rehearsal without Costumes] (Warsaw 1966).
17. J.P. Gawlik; quoted after *Teatr* 1976, no. 17.
18. A. Wajda: 'In Theatre . . .'

3. Andrzej Wajda's 'total theatre'

1. The term 'total theatre' is used here not as a historical reference to the directing techniques of Max Reinhardt or his followers but rather as the briefest – and most adequate – definition of Wajda's own approach, as described in this chapter.
2. A. Wajda: 'In Theatre . . .'
3. Dostoyevsky's letter to W.D. Obolenska, St Petersburg, 20 January 1872.

4. Marta Fik: *Rezyser ma pomysly* [The Director Has his Own Ideas] (Cracow 1976).
5. *The Danton Affair* by Stanislawa Przybyszewska was produced in 1986 in London by the Royal Shakespeare Company, adapted by Pam Gems and directed by Ron Daniels.

4. The dilemmas of liberty

1. Oginski (1765–1833), eminent Polish politician and composer, had himself to leave Poland and died in exile. *A Farewell to the Homeland* is his best-known musical work, epitomizing the nostalgia of an *émigré*.

5. Madness, love and death

1. *Zycie Literackie*, 1977, no. 8.
2. Private statement, 1977.
3. Elzbieta Morawiec: *Mitologie i przeceny* [Mythologies and Bargains] (Warsaw 1982).
4. *Zycie Literackie*, 1977, no. 8.
5. Maciej Szybist, in *Gazeta Krakowska*, February 1977.
6. Mikhail Bakhtin: *The Problems of Dostoyevsky's Poetics* (University of Minnesota Press 1984).
7. Unpublished statement made in January 1985. Speaking about 'most recent political murders' Wajda makes clear reference to the murder of Polish priest Jerzy Popieluszko in the autumn of 1984. Father Popieluszko, a spirited supporter of outlawed Solidarity, was assassinated by officers of the Polish secret police who claimed before the court that their action was ideologically motivated.

6. A reckoning with the past

1. Indeed, some time later Wajda has made a serial for television based on the same, though slightly extended, literary and historical material.
2. Zapolska (1857–1921) was an actress and dramatist, one of the first women playwrights in Polish theatre. *Mrs Dulska's Morality* is her best-known work, still a standard piece in Polish repertory. Its heroine, Mrs Dulska, the epitome of bourgeois hypocrisy, became a popular symbol.

7. Towards a theatre of politcs

1. Transcript of the interview granted to West Deutsche Rundfunk in October of 1984 (excerpt).
2. *Tygodnik Powszechny*, 1984, no. 5.
3. *Polityka*, 1984, no. 6.
4. Ibid.
5. *Tygodnik Powszechny*, 1984, no. 5.
6. *Polityka*, 1984, no. 6.
7. *Tygodnik Powszechny*, 1984, no. 5.
8. *Polityka*, 1984, no. 6.
9. Ibid.
10. *Tygodnik Powszechny*, 1984, no. 5.

8. Summing up

1. Peter Daubeny: *My World of Theatre* (Polish edition, *Moj Swiat Teatru*, Warsaw, 1974) p. 222.
2. The *Observer Review*, 27 May 1973.
3. At the time of going to print, Wajda's production has already been presented in, among other countries, Britain (at the Edinburgh Festival), the United States, and Israel, gathering enthusiastic notices everywhere. In addition to that, in 1986 Andrzej Wajda re-staged his adaptation of *Crime and Punishment* at the *Schaubühne am Lehniner Platz* in West Berlin.
4. 'In Theatre . . .'
5. Stanislaw Wyspianski: 'I ciagle widze ich twarze', a poem ('And still I see their faces . . .'), in *Poems, Dramatic Fragments, Remarks* (Cracow 1910).
6. 'Eklektycy czy doktrynerzy?' ['Eclecticism or Doctrine?'], *Dialog*, 1971, no. 11.
7. A. Wajda: *General Repetition* (Warsaw 1986; an underground publication).
8. 'Glowny topos Andrzeja Wajdy' ['Main Topic of Andrzej Wajda'], *Dialog*, 1975, no. 9.
9. 'In Theatre . . .'
10 Ibid.
11 Especially Chelmonski's *The Troika*, a huge painting depicting galloping horses against the plain, muddy landscape and dark, cloudy sky.
12. 'In Theatre . . .'
13. A. Wajda: *General Repetition* (Warsaw 1986).
14. Unpublished statement made in February 1985.

Epilogue

1. Tadeusz Boy-Zelenski: *Obrachunki Fredrowskie* [Settling Accounts with Fredro] (Warsaw 1956).
2. There is, however, an English translation of the play, under the title *The Vengeance* and in prose, by Harold Segel, published in his volume *The Major Comedies of Alexander Fredro* (Princeton University Press 1969).
3. Stary Teatr programme for *The Revenge*, June 1986.

Index

Abandoned by Reason, 58–61, 67, 69
All's Well that Ends Well, 3
Antigone, 4, 8, 9, 10, 102–8, 116
Apocalypis cum Figuris, 79
Art of Theatre, The, 117
Ashes, 8, 28
Ashes and Diamonds, 1, 3, 7, 9, 11, 14, 15, 17, 45, 68, 91, 92
As the Days Pass, As the Years Pass, 91, 95–102

Bakhtin, Mikhail, 81
Balucki, Michal, 95–6
Barrault, 51
Beck, Julian, 1
Beckett, Samuel, 62, 66; *Endgame*, 9, 62
Binczycki, Jerzy, 65
Bober, Jerzy, 16
Boy-Zelenski, Tadeusz, 126
Bergman, Ingmar, 1
Birchwood, 8, 9
Brando, Marlon, 16
Brecht, Berthold, 3; *Mother Courage*, 7
Brook, Peter, 51
Brustein, Robert, 112, 113–14
Bryll, Ernest, 108, 110; *Easter Vigil*, 102, 108–12
Budzisz-Krzyzanowska, Teresa, 45
Bunraku theatre, 37, 116

Camus, Albert, 34–5, 37, 81
Canal, 3, 7, 11, 91
Cat-Mackiewicz, Stanislaw, 82
Chaikin, Joseph, 1
Chekhov, Anton Pavlovich, 7, 11, 124; *Three Sisters*, 11
Chopin, Frederick, 13
Chronicle of Love Accidents, The, 11n.4
Conversations with the Executioner, 91–4, 102, 118
Craig, Edward Gordon, 17–18, 32, 117; *The Art of Theatre*, 117
Cracow, Academy of Fine Arts, 7

Cracow, Stary Theatre (Old Theatre), 4–5, 21, 24, 34, 42, 62, 79, 80, 83, 95–6, 101, 105, 108, 112, 113, 122–3, 128
Crime and Punishment, 8, 9, 10, 12, 69, 81–91, 98, 112, 113, 118
Cybulski, Zbigniew, 15–16, 18, 22–3, 16n.3
Czyzewska, Elzbieta, 114

Dance of Death, The, 33
Daniels, Ron, 57n.5
Danton, 8, 10, 56, 112
Danton Affair, The, 1, 4, 8, 9, 10, 49–57, 58, 59, 61, 68, 69, 73, 95, 102, 118, 121
Daubeny, Sir Peter, 112
Dead Class, The, 2, 10
Devils, The, 8, 9, 23–4, 28
Dostoyevsky, Fyodor, 9, 10, 12, 13, 34, 42, 69, 70, 71, 72, 75, 79, 80–3, 88, 113, 114, 124, 125, 126; see also *Crime and Punishment*; *Idiot, The*; *Possessed, The*
Dürrenmath, Friedrich, 29–30, 34, 113, 125; *Der Mittmacher*, 113

Easter Vigil, 102, 108–12
Eberhardt, Konrad, 20, 14n.1
Emigrants, The, 61–7, 69, 88, 94, 116, 118, 121–2
Endgame, 9, 62
Everything for Sale, 8, 9, 16n.3

Fabisak, Kazimierz, 42
Farewell to the Homeland, A, 67
Fetting, Edmund, 18–19
Fik, Marta, 49
Flaszen, Ludwik, 117–18
Ford, Aleksander, 7
Forefather's Eve, 3, 116–17
Fredro, Alexander, 126; *The Vengeance*, 126–8

Gazzo, Michael, 7, 14, 17; see also *Hatful of Rain, A*
Gdansk, Teatr Wybrzeze (Theatre at the Seaside), 14, 21, 55

133

Index

Gems, Pam, 57n.5
Generation, A, 7, 9, 14
Gibson, 22; see also Two for the Seesaw
Gombrowicz, Witold, 4
Goldoni, 7; The Servant of Two Masters, 7
Goya, Francisco, 58–9
Grotowski, Jerzy, 1, 5, 18, 50, 79–80, 113, 117; Apocalypis cum Figuris, 79; Teatr Laboratorium, 79, 113, 117; '13th Row Theatre', 18

Hamlet, 8–9, 11, 17–22, 28, 88, 91, 102–3
Hatful of Rain, A, 7, 8, 9, 14–17, 18, 22, 23, 28, 66, 112
Hübner, Zygmunt, 14, 24, 50, 92
Huk, Tadeusz, 106
Hunting Flies, 8

Idiot, The, 9, 12, 42, 69, 70–1, 80, 113, 124
Ils ont déjà occupé la ville voisine, 114
Ilza Ceramics, The, 7

Janda, Krystyna, 11
Jarecki, Andrzej, 23
Jarocki, Jerzy, 3, 4, 5
Jung, Karl, 78
Kantor, Tadeusz, 1–2, 5, 10, 117; The Dead Class, 2, 10; Wielopole, Wielopole, 2
Karpinski, Maciej, 94
Kazan, Elia, 15
Kepinska, Elzbieta, 22–3
Kiesielowski, 95
Konieczny, Zygmunt, 44
Kolasinka, Ewa, 106
Kordian, 18, 45, 116–17
Krafftowna, Barbara, 32
Krasinski, Zygmunt, 6, 116

Lady Macbeth of the Provinces, 8
Landscape after a Battle, 8, 9, 102
Lapicki, Andrzej, 32
Life and Times of Joseph Stalin, The, 94
Lomnicki, Tadeusz, 32–3, 58
London, 112, 113, 129
Lotna, 7–8
Lukasinski, Walerian, 48

Malina, Judith, 1
Man of Iron, 1, 8, 9, 10, 11, 21, 88, 102, 111, 127

Man of Marble, 8, 11, 21, 88, 102, 111, 127
Marat/Sade, 4
Mickiewicz, Adam, 3, 4, 6, 48, 116, 126; Ode to Youth, 48
Midsummer Night's Dream, A, 3
Milosz, Czeslaw, 13, 103
Mitterand, François, 57
Mittmacher, Der, 113
Moczarski, Kazimierz, 91–2
Morawiec, Elzbieta, 79
Morawski, Stefan, 10, 119
Moscow, Sovremiennik Theatre, 113
Mother, 4
Mother Courage, 7
Mrozek, Slawomir, 4, 5, 61–2, 66, 69, 94; see also Emigrants, The
Mrs Dulska's Morality, 95

Nanterre, Centre Dramatique, 114–15
Nastasya Filippovna, 8, 9, 42, 69, 71–81, 83, 88, 90, 91, 98, 100, 113, 118, 124, 127, 129
New Haven, Yale Repertory Theatre, 114
November Night, 8, 9, 10, 17, 31, 34, 42–9, 55, 61, 68, 88, 97, 98–9, 116, 118, 122
Nowicki, Jan, 37–8, 45, 69, 70, 73,. 75, 78, 123

Observer, The, 112
Ode to Youth, 48
Oginski, Michal Kleofos, 67; A Farewell to the Homeland, 67
Old Woman Waits, An, 4

'Pantomima' (Mime Theatre), 113
Partner, The (Der Mittmacher), 113
Pilate and Others, 8, 9, 10
Pinter, Harold, 5
Play Strindberg, 29–34, 112
Podkowinski, 99
Polityka, 105–6
Popieluszko, Jerzy, 82n.7
Possessed, The, 4, 8, 9, 12, 31, 34–42, 44, 49, 50, 51, 55, 57, 68, 69, 70, 80–1, 88, 90, 98, 112–13, 116, 118, 122, 129
Promised Land, The, 8, 10, 50, 102
Przybyszewska, Stanislaw, 95–6
Przybyszewska, Stanislawa, 49–50, 56, 95; see also Danton Affair, The
Pszoniak, Wojciech, 37–8, 50, 56, 115

Index

Rabe, David, 113
Radziwilowicz, Jerzy, 21, 69, 75, 78–9, 88, 123, 127
Reinhardt, Max, 41n.1
Richard III, 11
Royal Shakespeare Company, 57n.5
Rozewicz, Tadeusz, 4, 114, 126; *An Old Woman Waits*, 4; *White Wedding*, 114
Russell, Ken, 24

Samson, 8
Schiller, Leon, 3, 11, 18
Servant of Two Masters, The, 7
Seweryn, Andrzej, 115
Shakespeare, William, 4, 5, 9, 11, 17, 18, 124; see also *Hamlet*; *Midsummer Night's Dream, A*; *Richard III*
Shoemakers, The, 4
Slowacki, Juliusz, 6, 45, 116, 126; see also *Kordian*
'Solidarity', 13, 55
Sophocles, 5, 9, 11, 103–4, 107–8; see also *Antigone*
Starski, Alan, 92
Stein, Peter, 11, 97, 124
Sticks and Bones, 113
Streep, Meryl, 114
Strehler, Giorgio, 1, 7
Strindberg, 29–30
Stroop, Jurgen, 92
Stuhr, Jerzy, 21, 44, 65, 88, 123, 127
Swinarski, Konrad, 3–4, 5, 21, 42, 101, 117

Tabakow, Oleg, 113
Teatr Laboratorium, 79, 113, 117
They, 114–15
'13th Row Theatre', 18
Three Sisters, 11
Titus Andronicus, 7
Tomaszewski, 113; 'Pantomima' (Mime Theatre), 113
Tragic History of Dr Faustus, The, 18

Tygodnik Powszechny, 105–7
Two for the Seesaw, 8, 22–3, 28

Undivine Comedy, The, 116

Vallejo, Antonio Buero, 58; see also *Abandoned by Reason*
Vengeance, The, 126–8
Vinci, Leonardo da, 111

Wagner, Richard, 17
Warsaw: Church of the Milosierdzia Bozego (Lord's Mercy), 108; Teatr Ateneum, 21–2, 108; Teatr Maly, 9, 69; Teatr Na'Woli, 58; Teatr Powszechny, 50, 92
Wedding, The (film), 8, 112
Wedding, The (play), 8, 9, 17–18, 24–8, 97, 102
Weiss, Peter, 3; *Marat/Sade*, 3
While You Sleep, 7
White Wedding, 114
Whiting, John, 8, 9, 23; see also *Devils, The*; *Pilate*
Wicked Boy, The, 7
Wielopole, Wielopole, 2
Wilson, Robert, 94; *Life and Times of Joseph Stalin, The*, 94
Witkacy see Witkiewicz, S.I.
Without Anaesthetic, 8
Witkiewicz, S.I., 2, 4, 114–15, 126; *Mother*, 4; *The Shoemakers*, 4; *They*, 114–15
Wittgenstein, Ludwig, 125
Wyspianski, Stanislaw, 6, 8, 17–18, 24–7, 42–4, 47, 96, 97, 101, 116–17, 126; see also *November Night*; *Wedding, The*

Yale Repertory Theatre, New Haven, 114
Young Ladies of Wilko, The, 8, 102

Zachwatowicz, Krystyna, 52, 59, 83, 114
Zapolska, Gabriela, 95
Zeromski, S., 8; *Ashes*, 8, 28
Zinnermann, Fred, 14
Zurich, Schauspielhaus, 113